EVEN HESKEY SCORED

EVEN HESKEY SCORED

EMILE HESKEY

WITH DEAN ELDREDGE

First published by Pitch Publishing, 2019

Pitch Publishing
A2 Yeoman Gate
Yeoman Way
Worthing
Sussex
BN13 3QZ
www.pitchpublishing.co.uk
info@pitchpublishing.co.uk

A CIP catalogue record is available for this book
from the British Library.

ISBN 978 1 78531 500 8

Typesetting and origination by Pitch Publishing
Printed and bound by TJ International, Cornwall

Contents

This book is for my family. For the generations before me who fought hard to create a better life for us and for my present family who inspire me every day to always give my best. I love you all.

Foreword

by Martin O'Neill

FEBRUARY 1996. The rain poured from the darkened skies for most of the afternoon, so by evening kick-off time, Molineux, anticipating the arrival of opponents Leicester City, was well and truly drenched. Mark McGhee, the Wolves manager, had recently departed Filbert Street amidst antipathy and acrimony within the ranks of the Foxes who had watched a number of managers leave in recent seasons just when the club had looked set fair for better times. They were on the warpath, the portents were ominous. McGhee was going to get some 'verbals' that night for his hasty departure. I, as the newly installed Leicester City manager, had an immediate task. Don't get beaten by Wolves. And so Molineux, on that rain-sodden evening, was an intimidating place to be.

I needed a big reaction from the team. Up stepped an 18-year-old, with the strength of a titan and the pace of an Olympic sprinter to conjure an incredible performance that he would reproduce for the club many times over the next four seasons. Emile Heskey was that player. His two brilliantly taken goals not only won the match but made the footballing public take notice.

Twelve weeks later there were rapturous scenes at Wembley Stadium when victory secured promotion to the 'big league' and the young and extremely talented Emile Heskey was on an inexorable path to stardom.

He became a man that evening in Wolverhampton. His strength and pace from the left wing, his tireless appetite for doing the hard yards, plus an understanding of the defensive side of the game for one so very young, made him an automatic choice in the team. But actually he was a centre-forward in the making, as he politely told me just after our play-off triumph, and indeed, centre-forward was where he played for the rest of his career. In our first Premiership home game, on a balmy August evening in 1996, he overwhelmed Southampton with a two-goal salvo to introduce himself to the elite, a place where he truly belonged.

Quiet and well mannered in the dressing room, he was a colossus for us on the playing field. The esteem in which he was held by his team-mates never wavered, because even if Heskey was having a bad day at the office they felt that he was still capable of making something happen that would alter the course of the game. To say that we were an infinitely better team with Emile in the starting line-up would be a rather sizeable understatement.

With the club's growing success (four top-ten Premiership finishes and two League Cup victories, putting us into Europe twice) Emile's profile was burgeoning. And so it was with much pride but a great deal of sadness that I watched him walk out the Belvoir Drive training ground door and head off to Anfield, the home of Liverpool for a club record fee in 2000. The loss of Heskey was really tough to take, both for myself and the players. It left a void that proved extremely difficult to fill and the team, of which he was such an integral part, would soon break up, to take its place in the history of the club.

I am not well enough informed to talk about his Liverpool days, which were pretty damned good. Our paths did cross briefly in March 2003 when Celtic, the club I was managing at the time, played Liverpool in the quarter-final of the UEFA Cup. Heskey's equalising goal at Parkhead on an incredibly atmospheric evening was continuous proof of his standing in the game. Yet from a distance I thought despite an illustrious career at Anfield, more goals were certainly within Emile's scope. For some reason he wanted to become the provider of chances, rather than the goalscorer supreme. Granted, Michael Owen was the hero in those days and Emile's contribution was immeasurably valuable, but perhaps the shy, somewhat introverted part of his character had too big a grip on him then. Just my view. Emile, with some relish, will totally disagree anyway.

When I re-signed Emile from Wigan Athletic to Aston Villa some years later, he was a different character. A more self-confident individual, naturally, I assumed, as a consequence of medals won, goals scored and international caps gained. He was as physically strong as before but it was my belief that he had decided, long before his body had told him, that he could no longer do the hard yards. Maybe that was the reason for a blazing row with him at half-time at Selhurst Park in a tough FA Cup tie against Crystal Palace.

I felt that he should have got to the ball more quickly than he was doing, held it up better in proper centre-forward fashion, and certainly should have been in the penalty box anticipating the cross more urgently in the first half. He evidently didn't agree, and rose to his feet to tell me so with much more eagerness than he had shown in the previous 45 minutes. We agreed to disagree on this occasion. That said, my belief in Emile's ability never wavered, either at Leicester City when he was so young, or at Villa Park in the latter stages of his outstanding career.

Emile Heskey fulfilled his boyhood ambitions by becoming a top-class player at the very highest level; he has a footballing CV of great distinction. I now have the privilege of writing these words as a foreword to his autobiography and of all the memorable experiences we shared I still hark back to that rainy night in Wolverhampton where this precocious teenager lit up Molineux and, in truth, never looked back.

CHAPTER ONE

Five-One, Even Heskey Scored ...

I SAW Paul Scholes bursting through. I just thought, 'I'm off'. I knew I needed to run; to get towards the goal. He played me through. For a moment, the world seemed to stop. I just needed to get a good touch, to get the ball out of my feet and I'd be in on goal. If I'm honest, I didn't actually get the best of first touches. It was good enough, not perfect, but it didn't take me out of my stride.

If you can get your shot away early, it can be difficult for goalkeepers to get down to the ball. My mind was focused on striking the ball hard and low. The defender, Marko Rehmer, was closing in on me, and the goalkeeper, Oliver Kahn, was advancing. There was no space to go around him.

Keep it down, don't blaze it over. Hard, true, hit the net. I'd done it time after time in training, in games, but never on a night like this. And then it hit me 5-1 – I'd just scored in the Olympic Stadium in Munich to put England 5-1 up against Germany. FIVE-ONE. This doesn't happen. To put it into context, Germany had only lost one qualification game in their last 60 and hadn't lost at the Olympic Stadium since 1973.

I gave an interview not too long ago. I was asked questions about what I'd said in previous interviews in my career. One of the questions was, 'What did you say about your goal in Germany after the game?' I guessed and said I'd described it as amazing. Wrong. Apparently I'd described it as 'good'. Good? What was I thinking? I should have been on top of the world.

That's football though. When you're living day after day in that environment, the bubble, you take things with a pinch of salt. You're already thinking of the next game, the next challenge. It's not until you finish playing, when you look back on your career, that you take stock of those moments and your achievements. It's totally different to supporters, who will all remember where they were on the evening of the 1 September 2001; the night we put five in the Germans' net.

When I get stopped today by people in the street, it's the one thing that gets mentioned more often than not.

'Emile, 5-1, amazing mate!' they'll shout. I'll put my hand up, smile and then take another look and think, 'How old would you have been that night?' They'd have been in nappies, or at school, but it's just one of those games, one of those nights that transcend the generations. Something your mum and dad will tell you about, even if you weren't old enough to see it or remember it for yourself.

One guy once told me that he walked out of the pub the moment Germany went ahead. His son managed to get hold of him after the game and told him it had finished 5-1. He thought we'd lost 5-1. Everyone remembers where they were.

We didn't win anything that night. No trophies. We didn't even qualify for the World Cup that night, that was still to come, but we won the hearts of the public. We gave English football some pride.

Watching my goal back on YouTube, I'm shaking my head. I can't believe I had the nerve to tell Scholesy to wait, to let me do my celebration. Who does that? After the quality of his through-ball, I should have been carrying him on my shoulders.

I started to do my DJ celebration and then remembered I'd agreed to change it. DJ Spoony was the inspiration for it. He asked me to mix up my celebration and to do a golf-putting one. I didn't even play golf. I was in autopilot, about to do my DJ spinning and then you can see the moment when my brain kicks in and I'm holding Scholesy away, running off towards the corner flag. It was all a bit of a blur. I couldn't tell you what Scholesy or David Beckham said, even though they were the first over to congratulate me.

They played with each other. They had such an under-standing. At that time, Becks was just amazing. It was weird to watch, really. Observing football through the years, it's generally controlled through the centre of midfield. Becks was controlling games from the wing. He was a phenomenon, almost untouchable at that point in his career.

Scholes, because he was so quiet, no one really noticed him, but he was arguably better than anyone. He was like the opposite of Becks. Almost unknown outside of the game, whereas Becks was known worldwide.

These guys could pass a ball to you perfectly. Not just at you, but on to the specific patch of grass that you were running on to. If you were running, they would find you. It was a dream to play alongside them.

That night, we all thought back to the defeat to Germany in October 2000; the last England game at the old Wembley Stadium. No one wanted to lose that game and it hurt everyone.

I have a frame up on the wall of my house now. It includes my shirt, Carsten Jancker's shirt and it has the teams and score listed on there. I look at it as I walk past and smile. For all the cup finals with Leicester and Liverpool, the relegation decider with Wigan, and all the other big games I was fortunate enough to play in, this is the one that I'll always be remembered for. That night, that goal; five-one, even Heskey scored ...

CHAPTER TWO

From Highfields to Rod and Emu

I WAS a very quiet child. To the point where I'm sure my parents thought there was something wrong with me. I was shy. There are kids who go in to rooms and speak straight away, but I would sit underneath my mum's legs, looking around, observing. I came out of my shell through sports. I became myself. That and playing in the playground, any activities, but otherwise I wouldn't say a word. I was shy with everyone, even my own family.

I'm one of four children, to my mum and dad. My dad had two children before he met my mum. One of them, I didn't meet until towards the end of my playing career. It turns out he was a huge Liverpool fan! He might have been giving me some stick, without knowing he was related to me. We were three boys and one girl, a fairly big family, with six of us in one house. My dad's name is Tyrone, my mum was Albertine Newton until she married my dad; my eldest brother is Santana, then there's me, then my younger brother Revelino, who probably got the name I should have had given the football connection, and then my sister is Cora-Lee.

My grandad on my dad's side was the first to come over to the UK, with his brother, and they worked on the railways in Birmingham. From what I understand he found Birmingham too cold, so moved to … Leicester. Work that one out. But Leicester had a big Caribbean community, especially Antiguans, who were congregated in one area. On my mother's side, they are Barbudan and one of the biggest ex-pat communities outside of the country itself is based in Leicester. My mum and dad both came over at the age of ten, although there was a little age difference between them, so they didn't arrive at the same time.

I can imagine that it must have been tough for them both back then. That was a time where, for example, there were signs up reading, 'No Black, No Irish, No Dogs allowed'. That would have been very difficult to deal with, but I think in the long run they are probably stronger people for the experience, however unpleasant it was. Leicester wasn't always the multicultural place it is now, and they would have been some of the first people to come over, perhaps as part of the Windrush Generation, planting the seeds for us all to be here.

Our family settled in Highfields, an area right on the eastern edge of Leicester city centre. Highfields was the area for the black community and it was great. In essence, I didn't feel as if we had any problems. As I grew up there, we mixed with other black people, Asians and white people, but the majority were black.

I look back now and I was wandering off to the shop at the age of five, and to be honest, there's no way I'd let my kids go down to the shop at that age today. Everyone knew each other in the area. It was the norm. The guy in the local shop knew exactly what I wanted, before I'd even opened my mouth. There was a real community spirit about the place.

We used the community centre on Melbourne Road and there were a few shops there, which was all we needed: a groceries shop, a chip shop on the end which I loved, a video store and another groceries shop at the other end. My primary school was right opposite, Uplands Infant School, my first school. My grandmother lived just around the corner on Derwent Street, and there's a newsagents and a library there now.

My dad went to school at Moat Community College, and we lived in Pegasus Close, just off Maidstone Road and almost opposite his old school, right next to the main railway line that connects Leicester with the rest of the country. We lived on the top floor in a maisonette and I would knock for everyone on the way to school in the morning, and we'd all walk in to Uplands together. It was a very easy life for me then. Families all knew each other, and everything we wanted was around us. People went to the same pub, The Burlington, and my dad played for the Leicester Caribbean Cricket Club at

Crown Hills School on summer weekends, or we'd all travel to London to play against equivalent teams down there.

My dad worked for Rover in Rearsby, around ten miles from our home, north of Leicester and near the main road towards Melton Mowbray. My mum was in a hosiery factory in Glen Parva, in the opposite direction south of the city. They worked hard to provide for us kids, and that was the only way they knew how. They put food on the table for us. We definitely weren't rich, but I can never remember feeling that we were struggling.

There must have been some tough times and the 1980s were difficult for a lot of people, so my dad had a second job, as a doorman, working for a company called Starlight on the weekends and evenings. He worked a lot of parties and weddings in the Asian community. He would have found that hard. I can't claim to have taken that from him necessarily, but I always had a strong work ethic when it came to sport, particularly football, and from a young age I can remember never wanting to lose. At infant school, I would race a kid, and then challenge the next one, until I'd been through the whole school, through all the ages and beaten everyone. I hated losing. I was quick, very quick and I think that's when I realised I could compete in a competitive sports scenario.

I was taken out of my comfort zone around the age of seven or eight, when we moved out of Highfields to a nearby suburb, Evington. It was an upgrade but we were away from people we knew and people we loved, to a welcome that wasn't, at first, the same. Evington was totally different to Highfields. It was a predominantly white area, with a sprinkling of Asian and black people and it was tough to begin with. I'd come from an area that was perceived as tough, and on my first day at Linden Primary School, I walked in to the classroom, sat down and everyone was staring at me. This went on for what seemed like a minute or two, so I stared back at one of the kids and said, 'What you looking at?'

I understand it now. They were kids and they weren't used to seeing someone who looked like me. I had to come out of my shell very quickly. My early days in Highfields, around some tough people, had rubbed off on me and I had to show I was strong too. Even though I was shy, I knew how to stand up for myself. Our new home was 99 Evington Lane, and now we had a back garden, something we didn't have in our old place. We went from a two-bed maisonette to a three-bed semi. Mum and dad were in one room, Cora-Lee had her own room and then the three boys were in the third room. It was good fun. It was the norm and was never a problem. I'm not sure my kids today would understand sharing with two of their siblings.

I enjoyed my time at Linden. I was never any trouble for anyone, really. The school had its own small swimming pool, which was something you would never have imagined at Uplands, with all due respect to them. I can only really remember one teacher at Linden, and you couldn't forget him. Mr Turnbull was a tall Yorkshireman who had these huge thick-rimmed glasses, as he suffered from visual impairment. He would hold sheets of paper right up to his face, touching his nose.

He was fantastic when it came to sports. I don't really remember playing football until I went to Linden. Up until then I did athletics, played a bit of cricket but that was it. At the age of two or three, my dad took me to see the former West Indies and Leicestershire County Cricket Club player Andy Roberts and there's a photo of me with the great man. My dad loved cricket, but I didn't really enjoy all the standing around in the field and waiting to bat. I wanted to be involved and be active. I wasn't bad at it, but I preferred running. I looked up to people like Linford Christie. In terms of school facilities, I went from concrete to huge fields to run around on when the weather was okay.

Aside from my running, I still played a bit of cricket, tennis, football, basketball, hockey, anything. You name it, we did it at Linden. I can remember standing on one side, trying to hit the basketball board with a tennis ball, and we just did that over and over, for a certain amount of points. It was always Mr Turnbull who was there for sport. He even made us take cross-country running during our lunch break if we wanted to be part of the football team. We'd eat after, but before that we'd run around the main football pitch, down to the lower training field and back around again. It was only once a week, and people dreaded it, but I think it helped not just physically, but also in terms of building a mental toughness.

Linden's football team in my year wasn't very good. In fact we were terrible. We'd win a few games, but we certainly didn't win any trophies. There were probably two or three decent players in our team and that was it. In the year above there was a lad named Marc Joseph who went on to play as a professional for Cambridge United, Peterborough United, Hull City, Blackpool and Rotherham United, and was capped by Antigua and Barbuda. I played in his team a few times for the year above, but his side wasn't particularly successful either, so he was in a similar position to me. I guess that, mentally, it was good for us both as we'd have a lot of the ball, but we weren't guaranteed to win games.

I managed to score a lot of goals for Linden and used my pace to my advantage. Off the back of this, at the age of nine, I was asked to go down to train at Leicester City's Centre of Excellence. The best kids at that age were all put in the training dome at Belvoir Drive. The coaches would show us a few skills and then see who could pick up the demonstration well, and then we'd play little games. We'd do that twice a week. I honestly don't know how I got down there as my mum and dad didn't drive. There was a scout called Len Mawby who had spotted me and he maybe took me down a few times, given I was too young to get the bus on my own, or to walk that distance.

School was all about sport for me. I enjoyed my time in education, but I wasn't particularly good at anything. I didn't really focus in class as my mind was just on PE. I would count down the time; I couldn't wait to get out there and play. Along with the football team, I also represented the school in athletics meetings at the main stadium in the city, Saffron Lane. I held a lot of records, but I'd be surprised if I still held any of them now, especially with how people have evolved to be quicker and stronger.

I did the 40 and 60 metre sprints, along with the long jump, but I hated losing to a lad called Keith Garner, who was a couple of years above me. Marc Joseph beat me and that pissed me off too. I was never beaten in the sprints, but in the long jump I lost a few times. I beat one lad, Nathan Morgan, through the years and then he beat me at the end, on our last jump, and went on to represent Great Britain, winning gold in the Commonwealth Games in 2002. I still wasn't happy that I'd lost though.

Athletics was a major interest for me, as I didn't really play Sunday league football until I was around 11 years old. I know a lot of kids play from the age of eight or nine, but I just played for the school. Sundays in the black community was all about church and that's why I didn't play. I went every Sunday as a kid. Melbourne Church was near to my nan's house, and we'd all go to her house on a Friday night and stay for most of the weekend. If we didn't go to Melbourne Church, we'd go to the Pentecostal church in the town centre, which was my nan's church. If we weren't there we'd go to the church on Bodnant Avenue.

Despite this, I wouldn't really say we were that religious a family. My nan was, and she would be there all weekend, but for us I think it was to get rid of the kids for a few hours, to give our parents a break. It was like a Sunday school thing and then we'd walk back to my nan's, have some food and then walk around 30 minutes or so back to Evington. A parent of another kid at the Centre of Excellence nagged my parents to get me to play on Sunday, so eventually I joined Ratby Groby Juniors.

I knew nothing about Sunday league football. It must have taken around an hour to get there and one lad didn't live too far from me, Dean Blankley, so I'd either stay at his or they would pick me up in the morning and take me to the games. I'd never even been to Ratby before. They were the best side around, before I got there, and had some very good players in their team. Many of the players were part of what we would now call the academy at Leicester City, and we were managed by a guy called Pete Quincy. Pete would spot the odd player at the Centre of Excellence and would bring them to Ratby and strengthen the team.

I was so focused on playing football that I never really had time for girls. My first kiss was with a girl named Katherine Hill at Linden. We were friends in class and she used to help me with my school work. She was so intelligent and ended up being a lawyer, I think. I didn't have a clue what I was writing down half the time and she took the time to explain everything to me. Maybe if there was a different way of learning, it might have helped me. I hated having to stand up in front of the class to read something out loud, or having to stand up and answer questions in front of people. It was just a kiss with Katherine though, nothing serious as we were still at primary school, and then she went to Judgemeadow School and I went to The City of Leicester. She was cool and I always remembered how kind and helpful she had been to me.

As soon as the school day finished, all the lads would head down to the private Leicestershire Golf Club, sneak over the fence and play football. We'd round up so many of us on the way that it would almost always end up as an 11-a-side game, but before long we'd be chased off the grounds. We would play far away from the clubhouse, in a corner of the fairway, and the pitch was incredible. The best we'd ever played on. Then, when we were chased off, we'd climb the gates of Linden, from the Wakerley Road entrance, and play on the pitch there. With the goals still up it was much better than putting our coats and bags down as goalposts. Evington Park was free and available, but we wanted either a perfect pitch or the proper-sized goalposts, and no matter how many times we were chased off, we'd always come back and try again another day. We'd play full games, headers and volleys, knockout, all sorts, and we'd be on there until it was dark. On the golf course we'd tear the fairway up as we were all wearing football boots. They must have grown sick of us.

Santana was already at The City of Leicester, so it was natural that I would go there after Linden and it made sense for our family. Ian Thompson, who was a big name in local football at the time, also went to the same school. Ian's family are big friends with my family; my dad is Ian's godfather and his mum is my godmother, so we grew up together in the same area and he was three school years above me. He played for England under-16s and under-18s and was on Leicester's books, but tailed off a little.

Even today, people talk about what an incredibly gifted player Ian was. I can remember watching him score for England schoolboys at Filbert Street and he was unplayable. Then, of course, there was Gary Lineker who went to the same school as me, so that gave me some reassurance and inspiration. I was a little daunted by going to City of Leicester. I guess that stemmed from the fear of the unknown. Some friends went from Linden with me, so that helped. Again, I wasn't the best in class, but I did enjoy maths by the end of my time there. Like at primary school, I just never focused on classes, as my mind was always on my football, which I guess turned out to be the right decision. I mean, I made my Leicester City under-18s debut at the age of 15, when I was still at school. It was hard to focus on lessons when my pathway already seemed to be set out.

We were lucky enough to spend holidays in the Caribbean, in Antigua and Barbuda, sometimes for up to six weeks. We'd live out there with family and those trips have become great memories for me. I'd get to meet people I had never met and while the culture was similar to our community back home, the amenities certainly weren't. We had running water, toilets and showers in the UK, and they had a hole in the ground. We'd go off and fill a bucket with water in the street to wash, and the toilets, in the hole, were in a hut, out in the back yard.

I'd play 'kick the can' with my cousins. All we needed was a can, or a ball, and we'd be outside for hours. My mum's cousin must have hated having all of us there, with my great auntie next door, as we were in and out of every room. On one occasion in Antigua there were no amenities at the place we stayed, but we didn't care, we just made the best of it. I was a year old when I first went out there, but obviously I don't remember any of that trip. I met my great-grandfather and great-grandmother out there too, so they are special memories.

I was a normal kid in lots of ways. I loved watching *He-Man* and everyone said I was massively into *The A-Team* and I'd never be out of my Mr T jumper, but I can't remember that. There was normally calypso or reggae music on in our house growing up. Bob Marley or Beres Hammond would be on and I liked it. It was pretty special getting to hear that genre of music live out in the Caribbean too.

I still like that kind of music today. I have a pretty wide-ranging taste, apart from probably heavy metal, that kind of thing. I loved R&B from the 1990s to early 2000s as that was a really big part of my life. Television was so different back when I was a kid too. We just had the four channels and at my grandma's house I can remember putting 50p in the back of the TV and turning the dial to switch it on. We ate English food, but only if we went out to a pub really, like a Sunday roast, so it was Caribbean food most of the time. I'd eat pretty much anything, but Sundays at home were my favourite. It would be rice and peas, chicken, vegetables and dumplings.

It was even better when I went to my nan's. I don't know why, but it always seemed to taste better. I hated eating stuff like liver or corned beef, but you had to eat what was put on your plate, or you didn't eat at all. The amount of times I would nearly barf just looking at the liver and then just force it down me. I can still remember that feeling now. My kids are asked what they'd like to eat. It still surprises me when I go to see my mum and she asks what I want to eat. I just expect her to put it in front of me.

I didn't get the chance to watch much football on television as a kid, and it would depend upon whether anyone wanted to put the 50p in or not. I can remember having to sit and watch the horse racing, probably on the BBC, with my grandad. I could have pretty much fallen asleep every time and the same for Formula 1, but I do enjoy watching it now. I would probably be asking to see *Sesame Street* anyway.

I don't remember my interest in watching football developing until I started playing for Ratby Groby Juniors and at school. My parents didn't really have the money to buy tickets to watch Leicester City play, so the first games I saw at Filbert Street were as a ballboy, as part of the Centre of Excellence. I loved that, until the winter and then you'd sit there, freezing your arse off, soaking wet, sometimes in the snow. That was the worst.

I went to Luton Town to watch Leicester, with a friend and his family, and saw us play on the infamous plastic pitch, and can remember Alan Paris playing as well as Steve Walsh, who I went on to play alongside of course, years later. I loved John Barnes though. You tend to gravitate towards people who look like you and there weren't many black players around in the English game, but I loved him. I would pretend I could play with my left foot, which must have helped to improve my weaker foot a little, so I owe him a thank you for that as I did play on the left wing at times in my career. I admired Chris Waddle for his incredible skills, and later on I liked Ian Wright. I also loved watching Andrew Cole banging goals in for fun. I was a youth-team player when Andrew came to Filbert Street with Newcastle United. My job was to clean the dressing room, make the teas, pump up the balls, whatever I was told to do. Me and a friend forced our way on to working in the away dressing room, just so we could get close to him. I didn't dare speak to him, but I gave him a nod as I walked past. Being that close to a professional was like seeing someone from another world.

I never looked at doing anything but being an athlete, and then that desire became focused even more on becoming a footballer. There was never a chance of me becoming a teacher or anything like that. My childhood shaped me as the person I am today. It was tough and those experiences helped me cope with the tough environment football is. It's completely unforgiving and you have to have the thickest of thick skins.

Football can be a very isolated place. I was subjected to lots of racism as a kid and that developed my mentality. I've written a chapter at the end of the book discussing racism in the game and in society in more detail. I'd walk down the street and be shouted at. There were a lot of incidents within football and away from it and maybe that gave me the strength to succeed, I don't know. My childhood was an incredible experience though. I couldn't believe how lucky I was to live my life. I can still picture running out at Filbert Street as a 12-year-old for Ratby Groby Juniors in a cup final and pinching myself that I'd made it that far. We couldn't even kick the ball past the halfway line, but I was there at Filbert Street and no one could take that away from me.

Not many people know this but in 1989 I took part in the 'Emu Challenge', as part of *The Rod and Emu Show* on TV. You can find the video on YouTube if you really want to. My media agent, Ade Danes, tells anyone who will listen to watch it. Cheers, Ade. I'm there on the screen in a pink shirt, doing an assault course for the 8th Leicester Boys Brigade, along with two other lads, Darren and Ryan. We were on Rod Hull's team and I was introduced as Emily, which Rod apologised for, before later calling me Emily himself. From the look on my face, I don't seem best pleased. We beat the other team from Nottingham, who were in Grotbags's team and won £100 for charity. People still struggle with my name. If I go to Starbucks or Costa and order a green tea, I don't even bother trying with Emile and give them one of my middle names, William, instead. I've been called Emily way too often.

CHAPTER THREE

Growing Up Fast

THERE wasn't really one definitive moment when I knew I was a decent footballer. I knew I enjoyed sports and that my personality came out when competing, and if you enjoy something, then you are halfway to actually being good at it.

As a kid, I spent quite a bit of time on Evington Valley Road at LAYA, The Leicester Asian Youth Association, although there were probably more black kids than Asian, but that didn't bother anyone. I feel like I honed everything there. We'd play one-on-one, two-touch, three-a-side, you name it, we played it. That was from 5pm until 9pm when it closed and I was playing there as a 10- or 11-year-old, sometimes against 17- or 18-year-olds, even adults on occasions. We also played table tennis, table football, pool and arcade games, there was so much for us to do. We'd play Street Fighter and

Pac-Man on the arcades, and table tennis was really good for our hand-eye coordination, but football was what dominated our time.

I really started to love playing football around this time. If we weren't playing football on the private golf course, I'd rush home and then head to LAYA. My dad was there doing the circuit training upstairs sometimes too. There were some very good players there, and I feel like I grew up playing there. The games were physical and if you weren't up to it, they told you to go and sit down. I'd play now and again at the Boys Brigade on a Sunday and often that was against lads who were three, four, maybe five years older than me. Perhaps this helped me playing against older guys at the start of my professional career? For me it just became the norm.

I don't remember having a specific position as a kid. I just wanted the ball, played and ran around. Nobody could touch me for pace, so I was confident I could put the ball ahead of my opponent and then burn past them. People would give me the ball and tell me to run and I never looked back. Positions didn't come in until I went to Ratby. They asked me where I played and I didn't know what to say. So Pete Quincy played me at centre-back as I was tall, but I kept running with the ball into midfield, so he soon put me up front. Pete's son, Lee, played with me for Ratby and he was at Leicester City too and at YTS level as well. Brendan Davies was another lad who came through and he went to The City of Leicester with me as well. I was the only black lad in the team, but I was used to that. At Linden, there were only three black kids in the whole school, which included Rebecca Ndukwu, whose nephew, Layton Ndukwu, plays for Leicester at the time of writing.

I played for Ratby Groby Juniors for two or three seasons, scoring goals and we'd either win the double or treble each season. We were always successful, but then around the age of 14, I had to stop playing for them as I could only play for Leicester City. There were other lads I knew who had made it through to Leicester, like Guy Branston, who was in the year below me, as was Stefan Oakes who was at Aylestone Imps. Stuart Campbell came to Leicester from Corby, and Stuart Wilson had played for Ratby for a couple of years too. School football was totally different; you'd be lucky if you got eight players who were good, but at Ratby, the whole team could play and so could the likes of Aylestone Imps, who were one of our main rivals.

I joined Leicester City's Centre of Excellence at the age of nine and was part of that set-up until 14, at which point, as mentioned, I stopped playing anywhere else competitively. I think it was decided that it wasn't worth me getting injured in a school game or for my club side. I mean, it was great playing football with my mates, but with my winning streak burning strong inside me, I didn't miss losing games. I wanted to play with the best players, against the best teams and I wanted to win and break records. I suppose I missed playing for Ratby a bit, but it comes with the territory as you move up the ladder.

It never really dawned on me that it was getting serious, so I don't remember feeling nervous until I was playing professionally in my twenties. In fact, I was around 15 or 16, playing for the youth team away against Northampton Town at the cricket ground. We were 1-0 down after 20 minutes or so and I'm on the bench. My best mate, Owen Johnson, who was from Northampton, came to watch me with his family. The manager, Tony McAndrew, shouted over to me, 'Emile, come on, get your stuff off, you're going on.' I wasn't nervous, wasn't too bothered about anything to be honest. I ran on, scored twice and we went in 2-1 up at half-time. I sat down in the dressing room and Tony just started effing and blinding at everyone. He unleashed on them all. He pointed at me and told the rest of the lads, in no uncertain terms, that they ought to be embarrassed that I had come on, scored twice and I'd got them out of trouble, despite being three years younger than most of them.

The effing and blinding was just normal back then. Coaches can't get away with talking to kids like that now, but that was the environment I was brought in to. I've got friends who I think are still affected by the way coaches spoke to them back in the 1980s and 1990s. For me, I was lucky to always have this attitude that it could go in one ear and out the other. Maybe because I was shy, coaches and managers also wouldn't shout at me as much as they would with a louder character in the group. I was never really on the end of what others were battered with. In the second half, I played for around ten minutes, and then got caught by a defender's boot and came off. We won the game 2-1 and I never looked back. I played regularly for Leicester City at all levels right the way through from that day onwards.

It was a huge deal to play for Leicester City. Firstly, it's the only professional club in the county, and while they were a bit of a yo-yo club back then, in the top flight and then down to the second tier before bouncing back, there were always top players playing at Filbert Street. It meant a lot to my friends and family too. Every now and again, if I was doing well in my age group, I'd get to go meet the first-team players and speak to them, and that was another indication that I was on the right path. It helped that I loved training, especially as I got older. I actually preferred training to games sometimes. It was just so much fun. There would be so many laughs; we'd try nutmeg each other, someone would take a swing and miss the ball and the whole group would be rolling around on the floor laughing. These were things we couldn't do in a game. I would see a professional do something and then try to copy it in training. We were able to express ourselves in a way we perhaps couldn't do in a game, because of the importance of the result.

I finished school at the age of 16 and then started my first pre-season training with the first team squad. I can remember running here, there and everywhere, and the next day I woke up, I could barely move, but had to go and do it all over again. It was so tough. Mentally, it was a real battle to do that. We all ran at Bradgate Park, a huge country park to the north of the city, and as a younger lad I was expected to be at the front, but I started at the back. Halfway through pre-season and I was at the front. I'd applied myself mentally and my competitive edge came through. Running is all in your head. Your mind is what stops you, not your legs.

We also had a canal run we'd do near to the training ground back in the city – every team has one of those I think – and at first it was taking me 21 minutes, but by the end I was running it in 17 minutes, shaving time off as I worked harder to improve. We'd run out of the training ground, on to Middlesex Road, turn left on to Banks Road and then on to the main Aylestone Road before crossing over by the side of a school and then a jump on to the canal path and loop all the way back, including a steep hill run at the end. You couldn't stop yourself. There were 12-minute runs, as well as this canal run, and then there was a 40-minute run too. Most of the time we were just being sick.

I still think those runs have a place in football. I get that in a game you don't run for longer than maybe 12 seconds, and that there's a need for interval running to try replicate a game scenario, but I still think you need a base for your general fitness. Those runs and that discipline helped to shape me, I'm sure of it. It was a mental test to get through it, and then when we got back to the training ground we'd play a game, with our legs shaking. I can remember one year, we played a game, then had these runs, and then played another game within 48 hours. We just had to get on with it. No questions asked.

My parents didn't want me working next to them with the goggles on, or in the hosiery factory. They wanted a better life for me, which I'll always be grateful for. They wanted better for me, and I was good, so they believed in me. I knew in my mind at 16, maybe even at 15, I could play first-team football.

During that first pre-season with the first team, I got the chance to play against Notts County, but I picked up an injury from a tackle and tore my cartilage, which kept me out for nearly ten weeks. It didn't stop me from going out at night to parties though. I was wandering around on crutches, with my mum doing the cloakroom, while my dad was running the door. We'd be at Starlight, in Leicester city centre, near to where you sign on the dole, behind where the old Zoots nightclub was on Humberstone Road.

It didn't stop my focus on football though. I wasn't really distracted by girls, although I did enjoy going out and I saw a lot of my friends who all lived close by. At that time, a lot of my mates were playing football with me at Leicester, like Owen, who is the father of Darnell Johnson, who is on Leicester's books at the time of writing. Another mate, Brian Quailey, was at West Brom. I never got bored or felt isolated. Okay, my mates would go out and I'd have to stay in, but I was that committed that it didn't influence me.

I chose the right time to go out and never the night before a game. Maybe two nights before on occasions. It was actually quite funny to hear about the night out after I'd played a game, which meant I got all the gossip, without the embarrassment of being involved in it all. There were times where I was quite relieved to be out of it all, to be honest. When I did go out, it was generally to R&B nights at Brannigans nightclub, Churchgate, on a Thursday night, to a night called 'Sole Bangers'. That was *the* night to go to, so I had to sneak out to make it to that. I only went to Zoots once, perhaps to Krystals two or three times, but they were mainly pop or dance places, whereas coachloads would come to Brannigans.

I never really doubted my ability and no one ever told me that I wouldn't make it, or that I wasn't good enough. Kevin MacDonald was my coach at under-16 level for Leicester and Tony [McAndrew] was my under-18 coach, and it was only years later that I found out that Tony thought I was too soft to make it. Those views could have held me back, but luckily I didn't find out until I'd already broken through. Kevin was always easy to get on with, but Tony was very strict. I think that if you caught the wrong side of Tony, you might not want to make a mistake again, and it could make you question wanting to play football. He was tough.

I just got my head down and worked hard and was never really in the bad books. We trained a lot with the first team, which was good for my development, particularly in pre-season. On one occasion we were working on an attack versus defence training drill. I was up front with Owen; we knew what to do and he played it in to me. I then rounded the keeper and scored against the first-team defence. Players like Colin Hill and Scotty Eustace were up against me, as well as Walshy, and I had to use my size, even though I was young. They probably thought, 'Who the hell is this kid?' and I took a couple of good kicks back from them, which was just part and parcel of learning my trade.

Back in the YTS days, you'd have to clean a first-team player's boots. I did Colin's for a while and he was good to me. I also did Garry Parker's and he was great, but then Mark Blake, well, he was the worst. He was just horrible to me. He'd walk in to the training ground, first thing, shouting, 'Emile, where's my facking boots?' There was one occasion when he wasn't using his own boots; he was borrowing someone else's. I cleaned his and they would go back on to his peg. Before a game, on a Friday, it was one youth player's job to get all the boots ready for the next game. It was Lee Quincy's turn and after I'd cleaned the pair Mark had borrowed, I put them back on his peg. Lee went to round up the boots, saw that this pair weren't Mark's regular boots and removed them. On the matchday, Mark's storming around the place, screaming, 'Where's my facking boots, Emile? They're not facking here!' I asked Quincy and he explained what he'd done. I got the blame and I got so much shit from Mark for it.

Young players don't have to do any of this nowadays. I quite enjoyed cleaning boots and I felt that it helped to keep me grounded. I loved boots too. Garry had these £200 Asics boots, which was a hell of a lot of money back then. They were beautiful. Really soft leather. I would take the laces out, clean them, and then buff up the leather for him, and I didn't mind doing all that at all. I imagine that Mark perhaps had some stick in the past and then passed it on to me. Those guys got beaten up even worse back in the day, so I suppose I had it easy compared to them.

There were plenty of pranks in the dressing room. Banter as they call it now. We'd cut holes in people's socks and tie stuff together, but the worst was probably when we stuck a spider inside Stuart Wilson's sock, given he was arachnophobic. We'd tied his sock, so he thought that was the prank, but that also kept the spider in there. He untied the sock, mumbled at us and then put his hand in to the sock to pull it from inside out, and felt the spider crawl on his hand. He screamed and ran off to the boot room, locking himself in there. We persuaded him to come out, eventually.

The first-team manager at the time was Brian Little. I didn't really have any contact with him, apart from him seeing me in training a little, but John Gregory took the sessions. I was way back in the pecking order, as Julian Joachim was absolutely on fire. He'd been to the World Cup with England at youth level and he was being tipped for big things. He had the strongest outside of the boot shot that I've ever seen in my life. If you've not looked it up, check out his FA Cup goal for Leicester against Barnsley on YouTube. I think it won *Match of the Day*'s goal of the season. It was spectacular. It went like a rocket and in off the bar. He was a special talent, so I had to wait patiently behind him to get my chance, but I was still young.

There was a little bit of interest in me around the time I was signing my professional contract. The then-chairman, Martin George, said, 'If you don't sign this contract, you'll never play for the club again.' It was around 1994, and I've never spoken about it until now. I felt pressured into signing for the club. I was always going to sign. Leicester was my home and I had dreamed about putting on the blue shirt, but I felt the whole thing could have been handled a lot better.

I was a child and I felt like I was being bullied. My dad was with me, but we didn't really know what we were doing. It was all new to us. At 16, Blackburn Rovers were willing to take me for £1m. We played them in a tournament in Keele. Marlon Broomes played for them, as did James Beattie, and then we played Liverpool, so they must have liked what they'd seen from me. An ex-player was trying to persuade me to go. No prizes for guessing that they would have been on commission for the move had I left. That person retired soon after and became an agent anyway. But I didn't want to leave Leicester, I hadn't done anything yet and wasn't ready to leave home in any case. I needed to be with my family and I wanted to win things for Leicester and create something special. I couldn't have imagined how quickly both of those things would happen, but not in the way I'd expected.

CHAPTER FOUR

Leicester ... Where Dreams Come True

IN all fairness and I mean this without sounding arrogant, but by the time Mark McGhee had replaced Brian Little as Leicester City manager, youth-team level football had become too easy for me. I banged eight goals in three games and my coaches could see that I was too good for that level now. I was ready for first-team football. I was the size of an adult at 16, quick, strong and could play against older people; it wasn't a problem for me.

Mark had watched me in a couple of reserve-team games, and within a week I was training with the first team regularly and travelling to games with them. I was there to gain experience, to be around the professionals and also to help out the kit man and gain a feel for what it was like at that level. I was then pushed into reserve-team football regularly, and back then, in 1995, reserve football had old pros involved coming back from injury, and experienced players just on the edge of the senior side. It was tough, competitive and you had to be prepared to be hit, get up and get on with it.

I travelled to QPR in March 1995 with the team for a Premier League game, just expecting to do my job in the dressing room and learn a little more about first-team football. I was in for a shock. At the hotel, some of the lads had been taken ill and we were struggling for players, but I was just in my own world, focusing on doing my job of making the tea. Mark only revealed the team in the dressing room, just before the team sheet was handed in to the match officials. He turned the chart over and there my name was, playing up front for my home-town club.

I was lost for words. I was grateful he'd left it until late, as I didn't have time to think about it and get nervous. It wasn't a great game, we lost 2-0 and it wasn't particularly memorable for me in terms of performance, but it was a wonderful experience to make my debut in the Premier League. I was a 17-year-old kid, playing against grown men. The pace of the game made it difficult and the physicality was a surprise, but it made me realise that I had to get up to speed if I wanted to compete at this level in the future. I was always able to do that throughout my career.

A week after the QPR game, Leicester played Nottingham Forest who had a young Stan Collymore in their side. I was sitting on the bench and just before kick-off McGhee turned to me and said, 'Just watch what he does and then you do the same.' I didn't really know who Stan was, let alone have an opinion on him. He had a goal disallowed for offside, after lobbing the keeper from pretty much on the byline. That's when I started to take notice of him. I think we had pretty similar styles, although he was a bit bigger than me, but I always followed his career after McGhee's advice.

I made just the one appearance that season as Leicester were relegated from the Premier League, but McGhee worked closely with me as he had been a strong centre-forward himself. He spent time in training talking to me and showing me the kind of runs I should make and how to protect the ball from defenders.

I realised that everything I did at youth level had to go up a notch. Defenders and goalkeepers were stronger, quicker, better, and the reserve-team games were helping to ensure I was ready. I was still young, still learning and I was happy with my progress. I knew my time would come and then I could express myself properly. The QPR game had been a sink or swim scenario, and I was a swimmer, I knew that, but I wanted to reach the top in my own time and I wanted to be prepared for it.

McGhee bought Garry Parker in from Aston Villa in a swap deal for Franz Carr and Parker was just pure class. You could see the difference. He saw things before everyone else. In training I would make a run just knowing that he would play the pass. Garry would already know what I was going to do, before I did it. To have players like him around was just what I needed as a young striker. He had exceptional passing abilities.

We had a group of strikers at the club including Julian Joachim, Iwan Roberts, David Lowe, David Speedie and Mark Robins. I would watch Iwan a lot for the way he held the ball up. I'd only seen one other forward player who did it in the same way and that was Mark Hughes. Iwan would have two defenders around him, and would be holding one off with each arm, whilst bringing the ball down on his chest or thigh, and would then lay it off into midfield, or out to the wing, before getting himself in position for the next pass. His touch was immaculate. He was a much better player than people gave him credit for. If he'd have stayed longer, I'm sure he would have done really well playing in Martin O'Neill's side, as he liked to play with that kind of frontman. I watched him, learned and tested myself to be able to do the same. It wasn't easy, but with each week I was getting better and getting closer to playing.

Speedie, even though he was at the end of his career, still had the signs of a quality player. For a smaller guy, the timing of his jumps were perfect and he'd beat much bigger men in the air. He used his know-how, and I took a little bit from him too. Lowey was a great finisher too. He would score with the outside of his left foot, but would keep it low, offsetting it from just outside the box. He didn't get much credit, but he had a lot of ability. I was trying to soak up a little bit from each of them and then add it to my own game.

After the relegation, we started the 1995/96 season by playing a more expansive, passing style of football. McGhee encouraged his players to express themselves, to play through midfield and to run at defenders. Under Brian Little, the side was more accustomed to playing directly from back to front, but in Steve Corica, McGhee had signed someone who could play as a number ten. Add to that Parker, and then another new signing, Scott Taylor, who had bags of energy, and you could see a formula being set. Pontus Kåmark came in from Sweden too and he was very talented and reliable. We were playing in between the lines and were causing havoc for teams. We were tricky to play against and looked stylish too.

I recovered from a cartilage injury to make my first appearance of the season at home against Southend United in late September and then scored my first professional goal the following week at Norwich City. It's tough for managers to give young players a run of games, especially if they are under pressure to deliver themselves. At 17 it was a gamble to be playing me, but I was ready.

With just a couple of minutes left at Carrow Road, Lowey crossed and I was there to guide the ball home. Not a goal that anyone will remember, but a special moment for me and my family nonetheless.

I was then in and out of the side and in December, Mark left to join Wolverhampton Wanderers. I was grateful to him for the way he supported me, but I didn't really have an opinion on him leaving as I hadn't got to know him that well, or play that many games for him. Our first game after he left was against Norwich at home. Their manager, Martin O'Neill, had resigned on the day of the game and it looked as though we would appoint another of their previous managers, Mike Walker, who was at the game.

We had David Nish in charge with Walshy helping out and were 2-1 down when I came on as sub. I set up Iwan for the equaliser and then spotted a backpass by Rob Ullathorne and managed to get to the ball ahead of Bryan Gunn. I slotted home from a tight angle, in front of the 'Double Decker' end, for my first Filbert Street goal, to secure a 3-2 win.

It was an amazing feeling. I ran away as soon as I'd hit it. I didn't even wait to see if it had gone in. I knew. I look back now and it wasn't that certain. I'd watched so many players play at that stadium, but to play in front of your own fans and score, was something I couldn't put into words. David [Nish] had seen me develop from the age of ten. I was a month short of my 18th birthday. He told me to get on there, run at them and work the channels. It was what I always did.

* * *

If you watch the footage back on YouTube, you can also hear Nishy scream 'Emile!' to get me to run across the defence and receive the ball from Simon Grayson. He wanted me to show for the ball into feet, while the other striker, Iwan, gets into the box. I used this move throughout my career, accepting the pass, with my back to goal and the defender behind me, and wait until the last second, leaving them in doubt, before letting the ball run on past me, turning, and popping the ball across the box. For the equaliser, Iwan was there. I didn't even need to look and we were level at 2-2.

Martin O'Neill was appointed as manager a few days later and he had a tough start to life at Leicester. We were inconsistent. I was playing regularly under him, mainly on the left wing, but with the freedom to run at defenders and to join the attack. I scored twice in a win at Wolves, and two in a home win over Grimsby Town. At Wolves we were up against our old boss, McGhee, and were 2-1 down. I scored my first headed goal in professional football for the equaliser and then the winner late on as someone chucked a flask at me and Iwan as we ran away celebrating.

It wasn't always plain sailing though. Martin had a difficult run where he couldn't buy a win, and during the infamous home game against Sheffield United on 30 March 1996, the crowd turned on him. He introduced his latest signing, a loanee from Chelsea by the name of Mustafa Izzet, and it was clear that the City fans didn't have a clue who he was and weren't pleased about it.

That was Martin all over though; throughout his time at Leicester, he managed to unearth little gems who were either languishing in the reserves, the lower leagues or coming to the end of their career, and turned them into household names and Leicester legends. As soon as Muzzy controlled the ball and skipped past a couple of players for the first time in a City shirt, he never looked back and the fans realised they had a serious player on their hands. Coming from Chelsea, he had a good footballing background, but I'd never heard of the guy. I was very surprised that he didn't get an opportunity at Stamford Bridge, but we were grateful that this skinny little reserve was able to help transform Leicester City's first team. I say skinny, he had two little sticks poking out of his shorts that just about carried him, and his shirt hung off his torso like a tent. Boy, could he play though.

After the Sheffield United game, Martin met with some of the fans who had been demonstrating. I only found out about that afterwards. He took it on himself and kept the players away from it all. One of the best things about the gaffer is that he never forgets anything. So, when times are great, he'll be in touch to remind you about how you caned him when times were not so good. He did that at the end of the season and didn't let some supporters forget how they had treated him during that rough patch.

Martin has one of the strongest characters you could imagine. To go from that low point, to turn everyone around, to be successful and to go on and be a club legend takes real skill and belief. He liked what he saw in me and if he liked you, you generally would play out of your skin for him as he gave you confidence. He gave me everything; just relentless positivity. He and his assistant – and former team-mate – John Robertson saw something in me and John, specifically, tried to work on my game, having been a very talented and tricky winger himself at Nottingham Forest.

Despite what people might think, Martin was very calm at first. He took time to get to know the Leicester squad and the characters within the dressing room, along with having an appreciation of the magnitude of the job he faced. He sat me down and calmly explained that he believed I had a long, exciting career ahead of me and that I could achieve whatever I wanted. That belief meant a lot to an inexperienced kid. I always knew I had some ability, but Martin had the knack of making you feel you could take on the world. For someone of his stature in the game to give me his backing was wonderful. In later years, the backing would turn into dressing room banter, where he would take the opportunity to remind us all of the many trophies he and John had won under Brian Clough at Forest. We had nothing to throw back at him, but it was all good fun.

Martin knew exactly how to deal with you as a person; he treated you as an individual. He knew who needed to be bollocked and who needed an arm around the shoulder, and when exactly to do it. He gave me both; there were a number of times I was almost in tears and then the next day I was on top of the world. His timing was perfect. More often than not though, he supported me.

I was made to feel welcome in that dressing room by those players in the early days. Walshy looked after me well. I could put it down to my family being well known around Leicester, and the players knew who my dad was and my family. They would see my dad on the doors of nightclubs, and despite being a big city, Leicester is a small place, especially around the town centre. Everyone knew my dad and my uncles, so I never had anything to worry about. Even as a kid, people were shouting my name in the street. People seemed to know who I was before I was even known, if that makes sense. I was never bullied, or made to feel uncomfortable as such by the time I reached the first team and the senior pros looked out for me.

I roomed with Garry Parker and he was cool with me. Maybe it was deliberate putting an experienced guy with a young kid, but Parks was an absolute joker. He was a prankster, always up to something. Simon Grayson, or Larry as we called him, was another good character in that side. He dealt with a bit of stick from fans, and he was even booed at one stage, but ended up winning two player of the year awards during his time at Leicester. I thought the way he handled that showed real courage.

* * *

In the run-in at the end of the 1995/96 season, we only lost a home game against West Brom, but won three on the bounce, which meant we went to Watford on the final day needing to win, and results to go for us elsewhere, to sneak into the play-offs. Watford needed to win to have a chance of staying up, so there was a lot riding on the game.

Muzzy's header, his first goal for the club, saw us win 1-0 and squeeze into the play-offs. We felt like we had real momentum and Martin had given us great belief. We faced Stoke City at home first, which was a nervy 0-0 draw, where

Kevin Poole in goal kept us in the game. In the away leg, I broke through in the second half and stood the ball up to the back post for Parks, who volleyed into the top corner. That was enough for us to reach Wembley for the play-off final against Crystal Palace.

I know people spoke about Parks and Martin having a bust-up that season, with tea cups being thrown, but I don't remember that. We missed him when he wasn't in the side and he always made a difference when he was in. That showed that Martin was always willing to put the team first, over anything else.

It got a little tasty after the second leg at Stoke; I can remember my shirt being snatched and Neil Lennon was just standing there in his little briefs. We were surrounded by stewards keeping us away from the Leicester fans who wanted to jump on us and the Stoke fans who wanted to get at us! We were ushered off the pitch by security, but it was a really special night. I felt like we had the know-how and the determination to get over the line. Stoke were probably the favourites going into the game but there was no doubt in my mind that we would do it.

Wembley was an incredible occasion. We didn't get off to the best start as Andy Roberts gave Palace the lead with a shot that bobbled over Kevin's outstretched arm. After that, they had a couple of decent chances, but on the whole we were on top and always looked the most likely to score. Time was running away though. It's amazing how quickly time seems to disappear when you are chasing a game. With less than 15 minutes to go, Walshy played a perfect ball down the left and Muzzy didn't even have to check his stride. As he burst into the area, he was brought down by Marc Edworthy. Penalty.

This is where Parks showed exactly what I've been talking about regarding his character. You've got to have some balls to take a penalty at Wembley in a play-off final, with time running out, and against Nigel Martyn too, who was a quality keeper. That was Parks though. He just stepped up and got on with it. The place erupted when he scored, but watching it back on video, as the camera cuts to the sideline, there's Martin screaming, 'Get the fucking ball!' already focusing on us trying to get the winner. I still see Parks now and we'll be speaking about something to do with his coaching career and he'll say, 'Emile, if a penalty in front of 80,000 at Wembley doesn't faze me, then this won't.' You need people like Parks; cool, calm, collected. Pure class. He never showed the weight on his shoulders, even though he must have been feeling it.

* * *

We went into extra time and everyone was exhausted, trying desperately to muster up the energy to win the game before penalties were needed. It had been a long season, my first full one in professional football and that division is relentless; Saturday, Tuesday, Saturday, Tuesday and the games were tough, and defenders took no prisoners.

I was fouled in our half with a minute or two left on the clock and then Martin made a substitution that will forever go down in Leicester football folklore. He brought our keeper, Kevin Poole off and replaced him with Zeljko Kalac, the 6ft 8in Aussie, who Mark McGhee had signed earlier in the season. Obviously as he was big, Martin must have felt that he would fill the goal and intimidate the Palace players for the shoot-out. I was knackered and was just trying to get up after the foul and run to join in with play, so I can honestly say that I didn't even know Kalac had come on until after the game was finished. I must have been out of it.

I think it was Parks who took a long free kick and hit our centre-back Julian Watts, who nodded it down perfectly towards Stevie Claridge. Steve just hooks his foot at the ball, and you can see on the replays that I'm still a good 10 or 15 yards behind him, still not up with play. It was a perfect strike from Steve and gave Nigel Martyn no chance. He didn't even move. Time stood still. It seemed to take an age for us all to realise that we'd scored and we'd won. Almost the last kick of the game, the last kick of the season and we were going up. Premier League! I was speechless.

You'd have to ask the Palace players on the day if they were distracted by Kalac coming on, but it was an almost surreal 60 seconds or so, as I think they expected to be going to penalties. That was Martin O'Neill all over though. Everything he touched just turned to gold, and no one could deny that we deserved it. We had timed our run at the end of the season and we had wanted that promotion more than anyone else.

I get quite emotional when I think about that day. It was a hot day; I ran a lot up that left wing and had cramp on a couple of occasions. It was my first appearance at Wembley and my family were there. That meant the world to me. It was such a great feeling. I'd been to watch Leicester at Wembley a couple of years before, and walked down Wembley Way, towards the Twin Towers, so I knew what all the fans were feeling and how much it meant to them. It meant that much to me too. The whole of Leicester seemed to exit the city whenever we got to Wembley and the M1 was just this moving sea of blue. Our fans always seemed to bring more balloons, more scarves, more ticker-tape than anyone else. They really put a show on and I think we felt we owed them to do the same. At the end, it was all worth it.

The celebrations were crazy. My first trophy as an 18-year-old, and I wasn't a drinker. For some reason, I decided it would be interesting to see if I could finish a bottle of champagne on my own. Needless to say, the champagne finished me. We were in the dressing room, the showers, then the players' lounge, where I had a couple of beers as well and then the journey home on the coach and the drinking just didn't stop. We got back to Sketchley Grange Hotel, near Hinckley, and my dad was there waiting to grab me off the coach and take me home. The rest of the guys carried on drinking for another couple of days. Walshy, Muzzy, Lenny, those guys could drink with the best. What a party, but I was just too young to keep up with them all. It was a tough lesson for me that night, but incredible memories.

That summer, Martin brought the goalkeeper Kasey Keller in from Millwall and defender Spencer Prior, who he knew from Norwich. Kasey was fine, but goalies are always weird and he was American too. I thought he was a good keeper though, and he did very well for us. His kicking was his weak point, but he was a quality shot stopper. His weaker kicks would hang up in the air, and strangely that suited me as I could time my run to attack the ball and flick it on.

Spencer did very well for us too. He slotted in well and was a very solid defender. He would put his neck on the line and was perfect for what we needed at the time. We didn't have ball players at the back, we just had defenders who could defend. I scored my first Premier League goals in the second game of the season, a 2-1 home win against Southampton. The first was a tap-in and the second was one of my favourite ever goals, in off the bar, one that I caught perfectly.

I hadn't doubted myself. I tested myself and always had faith I could raise my levels. I can remember that game very clearly and Martin at this stage was just saying, 'Get it, turn and run, Emile, run!' It kept things simple for me and I was playing off instinct, without being too concerned about anything else. Later in my career, I needed to take responsibility and to show I had learned the game, tactics and my role, but back then it was just run and pass or run and shoot. I loved it. The freedom allowed me to have no fear of failure and I think it showed. If anything, I played better, despite going up a division. Our defenders were very kind and appreciative of what I did. They would look up, see me as an outlet and I would either win a free kick from their long balls, or run through and past the defence. It was the way we played. Martin didn't have much money to spend, so he had to make the most of what he had.

Martin did sign another striker, Ian Marshall. He was something else. Off the field, Marshy was just plain crazy. He was so loud. Everything was funny, everything was a laugh with him. He's a Scouser, so that was no surprise. On a Friday, in training, we would finish the week off with a game of young versus old. If you can imagine, these games were like the FA Cup final. It meant so much to everyone. The worst player on the day would wear the yellow jersey, which would stink as it was never washed, and had all of our abusive words on it. You could guarantee it would be Marshy or Claridge wearing that jersey. They were my strike partners, but they were the worst players in training.

Claridge would just be laughing and didn't seem to care. Marshy didn't train well in general, but when it came to young versus old, he would be all over us younger lads, trying to get into our heads and put us off. He was a wily old fox. He'd be in our ear, bringing up a bad touch or a poor shot, a bit like sledging in cricket, and before you knew it, we'd be wearing the yellow jersey and he'd be pissing himself laughing at us. What a joker he was. With the words he said, he'd turn the rest of the group on to you and then suddenly the whole group are giving you pelters. It was great fun. The games would be the likes of Walshy, Marshy, Claridge against me, Muzzy, Stuart Campbell and Stuart Wilson. The old boys, which in later years included Matty Elliott and Gerry Taggart, named themselves 'Smash and Grab' and they would just launch the ball forward, nod it down and score. That was their only tactic, no running, just launch and head. It wasn't football, but it was effective.

They would hold us down and you desperately didn't want to lose. We learned how to beat them by moving the ball and keeping it away from them. You had to take your chance though, as they were lethal in front of goal. We could have been playing against United, Liverpool, Arsenal or Spurs, but at that point, at a cold, rainy Belvoir Drive training ground, all we cared about was winning young versus old. Martin would come over sometimes and tell us to calm down, as he probably feared injuries, but the games were normally played in the right spirit. Going back to Marshy and Claridge, they may not have been the best trainers, but when it came to a matchday they were the real deal. They kept defenders occupied, were both great finishers and they helped me so much. I owe a lot to them both for the support and advice they gave me and I loved playing alongside them.

I scored a few goals, the winner against Leeds [1-0], the second against Newcastle [2-0] and we were looking up rather than over our shoulders as we adjusted to the Premiership. In November, we beat Manchester United 2-0 in the League Cup and Claridge's volley came directly from my back-flick to him, the kind of thing we would work on in training. I got the second, a half-volley after they failed to clear a corner and we were in the quarter-finals.

I think the media knew about me by then and they knew about the team and what you'd get from us. I was already playing for the England under-21s and we were confident enough to try things like that goal. I loved expressing myself. If I'd have done a back-flick like that at youth level, I'd have probably been dragged off the pitch, but Martin encouraged me to try things. I never wanted to do the simple thing at that age. I just loved the game and wanted to try all the tricks I could.

It wasn't until later in the competition that I started to think we could win it. Martin would have believed it, because he always did. That was him. Obviously you want to win every game, but we were all so focused on us staying up that I didn't pay too much attention to the League Cup. I'd grown up wanting to win the FA Cup and I would have loved to have done that with Leicester, but it wasn't to be. The media and the public all thought we were going to get relegated, so no one would have thought we stood a chance of staying up, let alone winning a major trophy.

What they said never bothered me. I looked around at those players and there was no way we were going down. We knew what we had and I think our fans knew too. Lenny, Muzzy, Walshy, Claridge, other teams would have loved to have those players, but we were unattractive. We looked like a scruffy outfit. We were a pub side. A bloody good one, but we were like a pub team. Normal, down-to-earth guys, who liked a drink, a night out, a bit of banter and loved to play football, but these boys never knew when they were beaten. They never, ever, gave up. Other sides must have hated playing against us. We were as tough as anyone, we worked as hard as anyone, we were big, we could head, we could fight and we could play a bit too. No one ever bullied us. Steve Walsh? You couldn't bully that guy. He was made of granite. I used to watch him as a young lad and that man had a magnet on his head. The ball was always his. Some people fear getting knocked out when they go in for a header, but he'd be the kind that would get knocked out, get up and win the second ball. He was incredible. Then there were others around him who would do the same. I could stand up for myself, but it was nice to know I had some serious back-up!

In the January, Martin brought Matt Elliott in from Oxford United. I didn't know a thing about Matt, but Martin paid £1.6m for him, which was a lot of money for Leicester in 1997. As soon as he arrived, you could see his calibre. He may have been huge, but he could play. His passing was first class, he could cross the ball, his touch was spot on and he could score. I can remember coming off the training ground knowing that we had a player on our hands. He was another undiscovered gem, who was a little older and the fans were probably unsure about him to begin with.

Matt also fitted in very nicely with the drinking school, so Muzzy, Walshy and Lenny had another drinking buddy to hang around with. I liked him as a guy and still do now. He was a giant and as brave as they come as well. A month later, we brought Rob Ullathorne in from Osasuna; my mate, who had gifted me my first Filbert Street goal with his backpass for Norwich.

Martin also brought Steve Guppy in from Port Vale. Now, and I mean this, behind David Beckham there was no one in the league who could cross the ball better than Gupps. His left foot delivered perfect crosses, and the stats would back that up too. We had big men and now we had a guy who could land it right on our heads. Boy was he nervous though. Nervous Norris we called him and he was quiet, a little shy, but he had some ability. He could drop his shoulder, without having to go past his defender, and he could whip a ball around the defence like no one. He just needed a yard and then you were in trouble. Gupps would socialise with the lads and would go for a drink, but pre-match, when others were relaxed, he was tense and anxious. He still put in a consistent number of performances though, despite this, and I loved knowing he was there to provide the service.

We were involved in a remarkable game at Newcastle, where we were a goal down, then 3-1 up, before Alan Shearer scored a late hat-trick to beat us 4-3. That journey back was devastating. I can remember asking over and over, 'How did we just lose that game?' That was the Premiership though.

We were growing in confidence and getting better as a side. We were such a threat from set pieces and Newcastle couldn't handle us, but when you have someone like Shearer, you always have a chance, and he made us pay.

Rob wasn't cup-tied so he could play against Wimbledon when it came to the League Cup semi-final, after we had knocked Ipswich Town out in the quarters, thanks to Mark Robins's long-range strike. However, poor Rob broke his ankle just 11 minutes in to the first leg, a total nightmare for him. He was a lovely lad. I sat down with him on a couple of occasions and spoke about his time playing for Osasuna and he said I would love playing in Spain. I hadn't met an English player who'd played abroad. The top players like David Platt, Gazza and Paul Ince had been abroad, but the next level down didn't tend to do that. As a young player, I just wanted to be in England and that's all I thought of.

We drew 0-0 at home and went to Wimbledon for a place at Wembley in the final. I suppose it was a similar situation to the year before, when we went to Stoke for a place in the play-off final. Martin had to be clever, as we had a few injuries and didn't have the biggest squad. We were in the FA Cup fifth round too and the games were coming thick and fast. We came back from 2-0 down to draw 2-2 at home to Chelsea, with a makeshift side and then came the infamous replay at Stamford Bridge.

I started that night, having missed the original tie due to suspension. We were absolutely robbed by Erland Johnsen's blatant dive, just three minutes before the end of extra time, and referee Mike Reed. There was no contact at all and we were all heartbroken as Frank Leboeuf scored the resulting penalty to settle the tie. We had given Chelsea as good as we got, and if it had gone to penalties, we could have beaten them. Chelsea went on to beat Middlesbrough in the final and their route through was winnable. Those years were when diving first came into English football. I'd never seen players dive as a kid, but now it was creeping into the game. It wasn't an English action and it happened as foreign players arrived. It must have been tough for the referees then as they weren't used to it. Now it's just part of the game. If I'd have dived as a kid, my youth coaches would have dragged me off the pitch and I would have been called all sorts of names. You just didn't do it.

Selhurst Park for the second leg against Wimbledon was an amazing night. I can still picture the Leicester fans down one whole side of the ground, making so much noise. Nights like that just didn't happen for Leicester. Yes, we'd been to Wembley in the play-offs four times in five years, but this was the League Cup, a major trophy, and in some ways we were not the most professional set-up, so it was incredible.

I mean training was good, but we were wearing Fox Leisure branded kit, a name created by the club to produce their own apparel while the opposition would be in Adidas or Nike. That didn't bother me, I didn't mind Fox Leisure at all; I'm just saying that we were a small squad, with not much money, a collection of rejects, and yet we just kept beating the odds. Our lads didn't care though. They didn't let anything bother them. It was an amazing time for us all.

Simon Grayson's brilliant back-post header from Parks's perfect free kick was enough for us draw 1-1 and go through on away goals, which we deserved, to face Middlesbrough in the final. Wimbledon were a big, tough side but we were tougher. We beat them twice in the league and knocked them out of the cup. We were made of stronger stuff.

Not long before the final, we played Boro at home in the league and lost 3-1. We were battered. Juninho absolutely played us off the park. He ran the show. And it was the worst thing he could have done, as Martin knew exactly what we had to do to stop him in the final. That Middlesbrough side also had Fabrizio Ravanelli and Emerson. I couldn't believe they had those players, but Bryan Robson had managed to attract them. No disrespect to Middlesbrough, but Juninho could have played for anyone in the world. I don't know how they got relegated that season, but they also reached both cup finals. They were incredibly entertaining, but also inconsistent and that's what cost them. Perhaps they needed our mentality? Anyway, Martin nullified Juninho by asking Pontus to man-mark him.

He was criticised for making the final a dull spectacle but what was he meant to do? Let Juninho run rings around us again? I don't think so. We weren't there to play our part, we wanted to win. Pontus was like a rash. A real pest who wouldn't leave Juninho alone. He couldn't beat Pontus for pace or strength and he was able to limit the Brazilian's impact on the game.

When I think of these big games with Leicester, I often think of Neil Lennon. He was without doubt the biggest moaner I played with. I knew he would go on to be a manager. He was an organiser, he was aggressive and he just wanted it more than anyone else. He was our heartbeat, the engine of the side, who just won the ball and kept it moving. At that time, the two best midfielders in English football were Roy Keane and Patrick Vieira. Right behind them, and on his day level with them, was Lenny. I'm not sure he got the appreciation he deserved, but ask his team-mates, ask the Leicester fans and they will tell you how important he was.

The final went to extra time. I hit the bar with a header in normal time, but should have kept it down really, then in the opening period, the ball has bobbled nicely for them and Ravanelli blasted past Keller. We were 1-0 down and facing defeat, but we just never gave up. Walshy was sent up front, and Mark Robins came on. His cross found Walshy, who headed across the goal to me, and I hit the bar again.

Then there was a mad scramble as Claridge tried to score, Boro couldn't clear and I stuck a leg out from on the goal line and nudged it home. We were level. I'd scored at Wembley, in the last minute of extra-time. We had a habit of doing that. I just don't think we ever accepted that we were beaten. If you watch the celebrations back, you'll see Lenny just standing there arms aloft and screaming while the Leicester fans go crazy in the stands. We knew we had got out of jail, but we knew we were going to win the replay. You could see it in Lenny's eyes. Those boys were winners and Boro didn't stand a chance. They must have been devastated to be seconds away from winning the League Cup, only to have to play us again ten days later. Our fans celebrated as if we'd won the cup. That was the feeling we all had. I saw Viv Anderson not too long ago, who was Robson's assistant at the time, and he said, 'Emile, that goal at Wembley got me the sack!' It must have been hard for Middlesbrough to come back after that.

One thing I also take a great sense of pride and satisfaction from is the fact that my grandmother on my dad's side got to watch me in the final, before she passed away, and my mum's parents saw me too. It would have been nice for them to see their grandson play at Wembley, the home of football. From their background, with everything they did for our family, I'm proud to have shared that moment with them. All their hard work and sacrifice had led to that moment.

The replay was at Hillsborough, and in the first half I broke through, shot across the goal and hit the post. We were poor in the first game, but always in the match. The replay was completely different. We dictated the tempo, the fans were loud and backed us, and even though it went to extra time, we were well worth the win and probably should have won by more. Stevie Claridge popped up to get the only goal and at the final whistle it started to sink in what we had achieved. Little, unfashionable, Leicester City had won the

League Cup and we would be playing in the UEFA Cup the following season.

I was riding the crest of a wave and I was playing a lot of football, including international games and summer tournaments. Martin and Robbo wanted to protect me and it was an emotional rollercoaster. I probably needed to switch off, and when I look back now, I know that they were trying to look after me and protect me.

The team suffered a bit towards the end of the season because of the cup runs, but then we won our final two matches against Sheffield Wednesday and Blackburn Rovers and ended up finishing ninth, despite it still being mathematically possible to go down with two games to go. It was as remarkable a season as we could have imagined.

Guys like Walshy were taking injections and tablets just to get through the season. He'd gone way past the pain threshold. The guy struggles to walk or bend down nowadays and that's the level of sacrifice he put in for the cause. He was a warrior and epitomised everything about us. We'd have taken 17th place if someone had offered it at the start of the season, just to establish ourselves in the Premier League, but Martin wouldn't have. He was always looking up. I'm sure he believed we could do something. I know he did. I'll never forget that season. It was magical and watching some of the games back has made me feel quite emotional. Martin and his ragtag boys had put Leicester on the map. Now we had to do it all again and take on the best in Europe too.

CHAPTER FIVE

The World's Greatest Pub Side

AFTER staying up in our first season in the Premier League and winning the League Cup, Martin brought four new players in: Graham Fenton, Tony Cottee, Pegguy Arphexad and Robbie Savage.

What can I say about Sav that hasn't already been said? Until you know him, chances are you're probably not going to like him. On his first day arriving at the training ground, he showed up in a brand-new purple Porsche. It said a lot about him, but I can honestly tell you that Sav is such a nice guy. I've got a lot of time for him. Sure, he's probably a little insecure and you need to reassure him and put an arm around his shoulder, but he has a good heart.

During our playing days, I felt that he could beat himself up a little bit and get down on himself. That's just his character. I had the privilege of playing alongside him years later at Birmingham City, and I knew his value to the team. Sav also knew his own value, his own role in any team he played for. He had such an engine, and no one could beat him at running. The Leicester fans loved him and the rest of the country hated him as he was a complete wind-up merchant. He would target the opposition's best players and would try to put them off their game. I wouldn't go as far as to say that Vieira or Keane at their best were bothered about Robbie Savage, but he gave every opponent something to think about. Robbie gave everything he had, all game long. When Theo Zagorakis joined us [in January 1998], the Greek captain who went on to win the Euros for them in 2004, Robbie was still more effective for the way that Leicester played. He epitomised everything that we were about; hard work, never-say-die spirit, lots of energy and playing up to being the underdog.

Martin had a unique way of managing Sav, which probably got to him at times. He'd pull Sav aside and say, 'Robbie, Robbie, all I want you to do, all I need you to do, is win the ball back and give it to these two,' whilst pointing at Muzzy and Lenny. Sav still had ability, but Muzzy and Lenny were ranked higher than him. He was actually very good on free kicks, but never really got to take them as Gupps, Parks, Lenny and Muzzy were all probably ahead of him. We were an established side by the time he joined us, and there was a pecking order. Sav was a young lad and while he may have been cocky, he got on well with people, got his head down and delivered for the club over and over again.

I didn't know a great deal about Graham, but he was a good finisher and I'd seen that during his time at Blackburn Rovers. I don't feel like he had many opportunities to play for us, and despite being quiet, I felt like he was a good character and when called upon he scored goals, and penalties in cup shoot-outs for us too. I'd heard that he wasn't too keen on Martin after he left, but then show me a player who likes a manager who doesn't pick them?

There was suddenly quite a lot of competition for forward places, which kept the pressure on me. Tony was a signing that really stood out for me. I think people probably thought he was old, here to pick up his final pay cheque, especially as he had been playing in Malaysia. They couldn't have been more wrong. The knowledge TC brought with him from his playing career helped everyone, especially me. He always said to me, 'Make sure you have a hobby away from football, as the game will drain you,' and I would think, 'Yeah, whatever mate. I'm young, don't worry about me.' It was only a few years later, when I was playing for Liverpool, that I realised how right he was.

We developed a very special partnership. We just seemed to click. He knew exactly what I wanted to do, and his role next to me. He has since said some nice things about me, like the fact that I prolonged his career for another couple of years or so, but he helped me immensely and I'll always be grateful to him for his support. We were almost telepathic. I remember beating Liverpool 1-0 at Filbert Street in October

1998 and the goal was so typical of us; me just rolling the defender, dinking the ball across the goal and TC was there to nod it in. I loved playing alongside him. There was nothing he hadn't seen and that made my job easier. I always felt like he took some pressure off me, as he delivered goals and I worked on providing for him. That was some £500,000 investment by Martin and if there was one thing he knew, it was how to get the best out of players in their later years. TC, if I'm honest, spent a lot of his time down in London and perhaps wasn't around the group socially as much, but when it came to training and playing he was spot on.

Pegguy was not a name anyone had heard before we signed him. He went on to become a cult hero at the club, signed for Liverpool, and also became my best mate while he was at Leicester. We are still close today. Pegguy was on trial at Motherwell, having flown to Scotland with his agent, with a view to getting signed. He trained, maybe played in a game, but they eventually decided not to take him. For some reason, call it fate or whatever, his return flight to France was from East Midlands Airport.

On the journey down from Scotland, his agent was calling everyone to try to get him a trial. One of the people he called was John Robertson, who agreed to take a look at this French international goalkeeper. The agent had failed to mention that the international part stood for under-21s. The agent really sold him to the club though, explaining that he was young, keen and agile. Despite not having played much, he trained with us and had a blinder, so we signed him. He wasn't the tallest keeper, but he had a good spring on him and was very good with his feet too. He did well for the club, despite not really playing many games, but he'll be remembered by Leicester fans. Pegguy was a good character to have in the dressing room too. He was encouraging everyone. When he arrived he couldn't speak English, but was soon involved in all the banter, talking in slang. He loved the lads, they loved him and he loved his time at Leicester. What a great signing he turned out to be for us.

Martin had let a few players go in the summer of 1997; Jamie Lawrence, Simon Grayson, Neil Lewis, Kevin Poole and Mike Whitlow. Jamie had joined under Mark McGhee and when you look at his life and his journey into football, you have to take your hat off to him. I'll always remember him in the gym. His body was something else and still is a joke today. He would come in and benchpress on the multi-gym and put the pin to the bottom and bang out 10- or 20 repetitions. One day though, even he was beaten. For some reason, the former Olympic champion Daley Thompson was training with us. He'd watched Jamie do that, calmly walked over and did what Jamie had done, but without even breaking a sweat. That was impressive.

We started the 1997/98 season like a train, beating Villa 1-0 at home and Liverpool 2-1 away. We were Villa's bogey team and that was for a long period. We just had their number. For some reason, we never really worried about playing them as we always seemed to beat them. Liverpool was a big game, especially away, but we were confident. I think that helped us for the memorable home game against Arsenal.

I don't think there's a game that defines what we were about better than the 3-3 draw against them. We were 2-0 down with not long left, following a Dennis Bergkamp masterclass. I got one back for us and then Matty Elliott got a last-minute equaliser. The place went nuts. We didn't give up and fought right until the end, but Bergkamp had other ideas and scored another beautiful goal, putting them 3-2 up in injury time.

It's got to be one of the best hat-tricks in Premier League history. On the first goal, I ran out to him to shut down the angles. He's whipped it around me and as I've looked over my shoulder I'm convinced it's going into the stand, but the ball just keeps on bending and ends up in the top corner. I couldn't understand how he'd done it. He was a little lucky on the second goal, but then the third was special. We'd bombarded them and smashed into them, but his class and touch was on another level. He watched the ball come over his head, while running and in one movement has knocked it up and then over Matty, before calmly slotting it home. Matty was class too, so it wasn't easy to do what Dennis did.

Most teams would have slumped to the ground. We had other ideas. We just launched it at them again and won a corner. Parks whipped in the ball from the right and Walshy rose above everyone to head it into the six-yard box. Spencer

Prior had the composure to head it back across the face of the goal and Walshy, who else, was there to bury his close-range header past David Seaman in the 97th minute to earn us a draw. Incredible.

Look back on YouTube and you can see the raw emotion coming out. It was a statement to say to people, if you want to beat us, you are going to have to fight us and go through us. Walshy, Mr Leicester himself, went running off and was pointing towards the bench. At the end, things kicked off between him and Ian Wright. I didn't see how or why it happened, but what I did see was that Walshy had gone. Completely gone. His eyes were somewhere else, like a man possessed. When Walshy saw the red mist, it was best to get as far away from him as possible. I mean run in the opposite direction. He would have taken them all on that night. I'd seen it before on the team bus, when he went after Neil Lewis for something he'd said, crawling across people, trying to get at him. Walshy was tough and so were we. Arsenal were an amazing side, who went on to do the 'double' that season, but we just never knew when we were beaten.

We carried on our good start, beating Spurs 3-0, and we seemed to have something over them too. We should have been 4-0 up against them by the time we scored our first in the second half. I got the third and the media were getting very excited about us. That win came just before we flew out to Madrid to play Atlético in the UEFA Cup first round, first leg.

When I think back to that trip to Madrid, I always think about their players. What must they have been thinking when they saw us? Ian Marshall, strolling out with his socks down, baggy Fox Leisure shirt and scruffy 1980s haircut. By this time I had played for England at youth level and under-21s, so I was familiar with trips to play abroad, but this was big for Leicester. We caught them by surprise, and Marshy was unplayable that night. His goal was great, tucking home from Walshy's knock-down. He was an underrated finisher and was that good with both feet that I didn't really think of him as left- or right-footed. It was a goal that shocked them.

Atlético had Juninho, Christian Vieri and Koke, so they were a top side; the hardest we could have drawn in the first round. When I look back at those times, we were punching above our weight. Saying that, we only lost 2-1 that night in Madrid, thanks to goals in the final 20 minutes from Juninho and Vieri, and came away feeling unlucky and that we could have beaten them.

I know we joked about being 'The World's Greatest Pub Side', but we could play. We were a pub team off the field, organisation-wise in some ways, and with our character, but we liked to play exciting stuff. Some of the lads went out for drinks after that game, but I stayed in. I was young and kept myself to myself. In the second leg, we were robbed. They were down to ten men and we were all over them. Muzzy had three penalty appeals turned down, of which at least two should have been awarded, before the ref sent Parks off for taking a free kick too quickly.

We lost 2-0 and I thought Martin was going to explode afterwards. I'd never seen him so angry. The ref, a French guy called Remi Harrel, was disciplined by UEFA and didn't referee in the UEFA Cup again that season. We were all gutted. The atmosphere that night was out of this world; the balloons, the ticker-tape, the noise. It was a different atmosphere that evening. I think maybe as the Leicester fans had been starved of that kind of football for so long, they just went for it. I never played for the club again in Europe as I'd left by the time the team played Red Star Belgrade in 2000; and although it might have only been two games in Europe, what a journey it was for us. I'd gone from the second tier, to a Wembley play-off win, then a League Cup win and top-ten finish, to then running Atlético Madrid close. What a remarkable time it was for the club. I think we allowed the people of Leicester to dream again and believe in their club.

I was sent off for the first time in my career in a 3-3 draw at Newcastle that November. We often seemed to have epic games against them as they were an entertaining, attacking side. The red card was a scuffle. Philippe Albert grabbed me, I grappled with him and then I raised my arms and pushed him away. I wasn't trying to hurt him or hit him, it was nothing really, but once you do that and the fans start calling for the ref to send you off, at a place like that, then you are risking it. It was stupid and I was gutted to leave the field. I wasn't a dirty player at all, I was just physical. I never went out on to the field to hurt anyone, or elbow them or anything like that.

Another memorable performance that season was beating Manchester United 1-0 at Old Trafford at the end of January, thanks to TC, who flicked the ball past Peter Schmeichel. That was an incredibly tough place to go at that time and hardly anyone got anything there. I scored both in a 2-0 win at home to Chelsea, another big club who we tended to do well against. We were never a side that would play out from the back; our defenders knew how to defend and our midfield was quality. We had excellent game management skills and knew when to play and when to just dig in. Generally, teams didn't like to play against us, especially at Filbert Street. They knew they would be in a game against us.

With TC doing so well and Marshy still a threat, my old strike partner Stevie Claridge left in the January. He did something so special for Leicester. We wouldn't have reached the Premier League without him and he won us the League Cup too. Two iconic goals in the space of a year means he'll always be a hero in Leicester. He brought so much happiness to the club and the fans still sing about him. His impact was incredible. He was so good at hold-up play and was underrated. I was honoured to have played alongside him. I know he could be a mess to look at on the pitch, but I loved having him next to me. So did guys like Muzzy and Gupps, who would receive the ball off him. Stevie was something else for Leicester and will forever be written into the club's history as a true hero.

Towards the end of the season we were involved in a game that no Leicester fan will ever forget. We won 4-0 away at local rivals, Derby County, with all four goals being headers and all four coming in the first 15 minutes.

I got the first and third, Muzzy the second, and Marshy the fourth. We were rampant. The delivery was perfect and we were so effective at crossing and getting a header on target. Arsène Wenger once described us as 'the best set-piece side in Europe' and he was right. We didn't particularly have a tactic for them though. It was all based on getting the ball in the danger area and then our big men getting their head on it.

The Derby fans were shell-shocked and some of them walked out after the fourth goal. Three days later we drew 0-0 at home to Newcastle and that ended any chance we had of qualifying for Europe through the league. The game will always be remembered for Alan Shearer kicking Neil Lennon in the face, by the touchline. I've watched it back and I don't think there's any way you can defend him. It was a clear red card and I'm not sure how he got away with it. His left boot moved in a way that suggests he kicked out at Lenny. If he was trying to move his foot away, then it would have gone away from Lenny's head, not towards it. It was an unsavoury incident and I think Shearer was lucky it happened then, back in 1998, and not today, as he'd have received a serious ban.

That summer, Martin strengthened the squad again. He let Julian Watts and Spencer Prior leave, who had both been solid for us, and brought in Gerry Taggart and Frank

Sinclair. They both settled in very well, very well indeed, as they absolutely loved a drink. Walshy, Lenny, Muzzy and Matty loved these two joining as it added another two to the drinking school. Taggs used to have his cousin come on nights out, or on trips away, and they would sit in the bar, playing the guitar, singing Irish songs and they would fill the room with empty bottles and drink the place dry. It was ridiculous. Those boys could put it away, but come training and game day, they would be on the ball.

Taggs was a superb threat at set pieces. He was brought in as competition for Walshy, who had suffered with injuries and was getting older, but they both played at times and Taggs never let us down. I think he found it difficult at first though, as we never messed around with the ball at the back, and he would want to play the ball out. Martin found it difficult with him too, but Taggs got his head down and did what the manager needed and he flourished.

Frank was great for us too, as the one thing we needed was pace at the back. He could play in the back three, or as a right wing-back and he helped out massively. He offered cover to the other guys and I don't think he got as much credit as he deserved because he joined after some of our success. The other defenders like Matty and Walshy are thought of as the heroes at the back, so it was tough for Frank to get that level of recognition.

He was crazy though. He loved his drink. I'm sure he was out nearly every night of the week. He was such a sociable guy.

He moved up from London to Leicester and loved it in the city, but I reckon Friday night was the only night he stayed in. He loved having people around him, whereas I liked some quiet time and enjoyed being at home, comfortable in my own company. I couldn't keep up with them back then and I was never really a big drinker anyway. Nowadays I'm even worse. One night out and I need a month to recover.

We started the 1998/99 season at Old Trafford. It was just after the France World Cup and David Beckham's sending off against Argentina for his soft kick on Diego Simeone. I scored early and we were 2-0 up late on, but Teddy Sheringham got one back with 11 minutes left and then Beckham scored a great free kick in injury time to get them a 2-2 draw. It was just weeks after effigies of Becks were being hung outside of pubs and there he was, doing what he did best. It showed the character of the man and just a couple of years later he was captaining his country. That was such a low point for him against Argentina. It was never a red card in my eyes, only a yellow card, but that's football.

He came a long way in such a short time and it showed how far we had come too, for little Leicester to be disappointed at only drawing away to Manchester United. That was the season they went on to win the treble and there we were, taking them right to the wire. They were the best of the best.

We were all really down afterwards, which was a far cry from the season before, when we beat them 1-0 with TC's goal. I remember Martin came back into the dressing room on cloud nine. He was high-fiving everyone, hugging us all. He could be quite erratic in his behaviour, and he was bouncing around the room. Marshy, who being a Scouser had a cheeky side to him, shouted out, 'Days off? See you on Thursday?' and Martin heard it and replied, 'You want days off? No problem. You're all off until Thursday.' He was so desperate for us all to be happy that he agreed straight away and Marshy had got his wish. Martin understood people so well and was such a great man-manager. I could have probably done with more training, but it didn't really matter as Martin kept everyone happy.

It was no surprise that clubs were interested in taking him away from us. Everton, Spurs and Leeds had all been linked and when Leeds made an approach, after George Graham left them, it created an emotional night at Filbert Street. We played Spurs on a Monday evening in October and the local newspaper, the *Leicester Mercury*, printed banners saying the words 'Don't Go Martin' and handed them to the fans outside the ground, who held them up as the teams came out. I'd never seen anything like that. Generally, newspapers don't tend to go that far, to be that behind one man. He was the king of the city. The people loved him.

He kept the speculation away from us and I just got on with my game. We beat Tottenham 2-1. I got our first, by rolling Ramon Vega with a goal I loved, very typical of my style of play at that time, and then a stunning volley from Muzzy, five minutes from time. The place erupted. I know that Martin felt very touched by the outpouring of emotion towards him and it helped to persuade him to stay. I always believed he would stay as we were on a roll and the momentum we had made me believe we could go on and achieve more. Anything was possible with Martin. At this time, I never felt the need to leave myself. We were riding on a wave which was going higher and higher. As players, I don't ever remember us having to ask Martin to stay. I think he felt that the project at Leicester was incomplete and that to leave would have been a gamble in itself as he'd worked so hard to build something.

Soon after, we disposed of Liverpool again, 1-0 at home with the TC header I mentioned earlier, after I'd rolled the defender and crossed for him instinctively. On *Match of the Day*, Alan Hansen talked up the likes of myself, Muzzy, Lenny and Matty as being good enough to play for Liverpool and Martin, needless to say, wasn't happy about his players being touted for a bigger club. As football would have it, we drew Leeds at home in the League Cup fourth round, which gave their fans the chance to sing, 'Martin O'Neill, stay with Leicester City and you'll win fuck all!'

They couldn't have been more wrong, and it probably showed that while they had David O'Leary, who did well there, he was no Martin O'Neill. Kasey Keller made a mistake which put them ahead. Kasey was a good keeper overall, but as I mentioned earlier, his kicking was poor. He could also be a bit of a shithouse when it came to claiming crosses, but as I've said he was a quality shot stopper.

Robert Molenaar, who was a complete fucking tank, kicked lumps out of us that night. I went off injured after a tackle by Jonathan Woodgate and with TC injured and other strikers out, we had Walshy playing up front and then Matty joined him at the end. We were finishing the game with two centre-backs as centre-forward, but those boys loved the chance to go up front. It was Muzzy who equalised with a minute to go, with an incredible lob from distance after Nigel Martyn came rushing out to head it. Then, just a minute later, Muzzy burst into the area and was fouled by Molenaar, leaving Parks to face Martyn from the spot, as he had done at Wembley in the play-off final against Crystal Palace. The end result was the same and we were in the quarter-finals. It was smash and grab, but we just never knew when we were beaten.

After getting past Blackburn Rovers in the quarters, we faced Sunderland over two legs in the semi-finals. Sunderland were flying high at the top of the second tier and were a Premier League side in all but name. We went up there first and TC got two goals and we were comfortable before conceding a late goal. In the second leg, Niall Quinn put them ahead, so we were 2-2 on aggregate.

Martin absolutely roasted us at half-time and brought Sav on, who got the crowd going and helped to up the tempo. We were the better side in the second half and TC scored his third goal of the tie, to take us to Wembley again. It was an amazing feeling. In four seasons at the club, we were now set to make our third Wembley appearance.

In the build-up to the final against Spurs, I was suffering with a bad back. I was in agony. I eventually found out that it was being caused by a muscle imbalance, and my lower back muscles were taking over and seizing up. I was suffering from spasms and couldn't move. We did a shooting session in training for five minutes and I had to stop and lie down in the foetal position, which was the only way I felt comfortable. Martin thought I was messing around but it was serious. In order to play at Wembley, I had to take injections, but they didn't work. If I was 100 per cent fit for that game, we would have won that final.

I don't want that to sound arrogant, but I wasn't even close to being fit, and I fancied myself against that Spurs side. I think the gaffer understood after the game just how much pain I was in. The way we were structured at that time, I had to play. I was so upset. When you get to a Wembley final you want to be able to show people what you can do.

My back was eventually sorted after visiting physiotherapists in Loughborough, and I saw a woman called Judith, and Dave Rennie, who became the club's physio, and they had a week to fix me. My groins, glutes and hip muscles weren't working properly, so they reprogrammed my body and got me back to fitness and in shape. That came a week too late for the final.

The game itself was cagey. We rarely talked about opposition sides, maybe only Arsenal who were a huge threat, but we beat everyone else. I went through on goal, but couldn't get away because of my back. TC came close and then the key moment in the match; Justin Edinburgh, whose passing earlier this year shocked us all, was sent off for raising his hands to Sav, who'd flown in on Edinburgh with his initial challenge. We had the extra man and were favourites to win it, but Spurs nicked a last-minute goal and we didn't have time to reply. It was an awful feeling. I'd already been subbed off by then and everyone remembers the tears of TC at the end, who must have felt that his last chance of a winners' medal had passed him by. Little did he know what was to come just 12 months later.

Sav's dust-up wasn't the only controversy that day. Frank was left out for missing a team meeting. I don't remember the incident happening, but that was what we were told. Then there was crowd trouble during the game, with Spurs fans having access to tickets in the Leicester end and some of those tickets were allegedly the ones that players had. I knew they weren't mine. My tickets went to family and friends so it was all Leicester fans. I bought my tickets and passed them on to family, and could have done with more such was the demand. A few of the lads and some of the staff were banned from having access to tickets for a period after this. It was made worse by pictures of a poor woman being attacked by a thug. That final left a bitter taste in everyone's mouths.

A couple of weeks later, we were at White Hart Lane to play Spurs in the league. Martin had arranged for us all to give them a guard of honour and hand out bouquets of flowers to each player. It was exactly the kind of psychological thing he liked to do. He wanted the Spurs players to feel that we were beaten and would lie down and let them win again. There was no chance of that. It may have come two weeks too late, but we smashed into them, winning 2-0. I don't know if the flowers made any difference, but I just wanted to make up for the Wembley defeat. Matty got the first and TC the second goal. After his tears at Wembley, this result wouldn't make up for the disappointment but underlined what a true professional TC was. I was just pleased to be able to run freely again. That completed our double over them in the league, but it still pisses me off that I wasn't fit for Wembley.

Ever since I'd burst through at Leicester, the fans had called me 'Bruno' after the boxer Frank Bruno, who was a household name. Like him, I was big, powerful and black. I was never called Bruno anywhere else. I didn't get a choice in the matter but it didn't really bother me. In fact, some of the lads still call me Bruno. If I'm being honest, I would rather have been known for my own name, not Frank's, but it wasn't a big deal.

Times have changed and I think as a young lad back then, you'd just have to take the name. Nowadays, young lads would feel more confident in rejecting it. I was proud of the fact that the fans were chanting for me. I didn't want Leicester fans to think that I didn't like it or that I was offended. I wasn't. I just wanted to be known as a footballer, not as a black boxer. I look nothing like him, but I don't blame anyone for calling me it. The name just stuck. I never made a fuss about it. I loved playing for Leicester and I loved the fans and that relationship will always be special to me.

In the summer of 1999, my final season with Leicester, Martin made a signing that turned out to be one of the best he ever made, in my opinion, Tim Flowers. He was a great goalkeeper. David Seaman always signed his name with 'Safe Hands' underneath it, well, Tim should have done that as well. He was absolutely brilliant. Incredible. Leicester have had some first-class goalkeepers down the years including the late Gordon Banks, Peter Shilton and now Kasper Schmeichel, and Tim would be up there with them.

He was older and wiser by the time he joined us. I thought of him as a sensible bloke, who never really got too involved in the drinking culture and was just an excellent professional. As a result of Tim's arrival, Kasey left us. He went on to play at Spurs, in Spain and continued to represent the US national team. He had a great career.

Phil Gilchrist joined as a back-up defender; he was a quiet lad, had a good left foot and did well when he was called upon. Scott Taylor and Guy Branston left during this season too. Guy was at the club at a difficult time, as there were so many good centre-backs ahead of him and he was young. He was a no-nonsense defender; he knew his role and his limitations, and went on to have a very good career. In all fairness, he wasn't great on the ball, but you couldn't beat him for effort and for his actual defensive abilities. He dropped down the leagues and built himself back up. I played against him in the cup for Liverpool and he was a battler. He never gave up. He went on to have a good career and is well-respected in the football community.

We opened the season with a 2-1 defeat at Arsenal, thanks in no small part to Frank's late headed own-goal. A week later, we were 2-1 up at home to Chelsea, before Frank's head popped up again and equalised for them in injury time. It didn't seem possible for the ball to come off his head the way it did on both occasions. The lads were gutted and gutted for him. I was too young to be able to take the piss out of him. Marshy would have said something, I'm sure. After I'd left, Frank also scored an own goal from just inside his own half when playing for Leicester against Middlesbrough – what a hat-trick! In all seriousness though, he was quality for us and I loved playing with him.

In December we signed Darren Eadie from Norwich City. Darren was desperately unlucky with injuries and it never really happened for him at Leicester. Martin knew him from Norwich; he had pace to burn. He was so quick. Injuries are an interesting thing. Everyone gets them, but he was just so unlucky. Who do you blame for that? He was very talented, and Martin got almost all of his signings right, but you can't control things like that, really.

I didn't want this book to be me just talking through each game I played in, but this season was remarkable for the fact that we ended up having three penalty shoot-outs, winning all of them. We drew 0-0 with Leeds United in the League Cup fourth round and beat them 4-2 on penalties. In the next round, we drew 3-3 with Fulham and won 3-0 on penalties, and then a week later, we drew 0-0 with Arsenal in the FA Cup, in a replay, and beat them 6-5 on penalties. All of these were at home and they were all magical nights.

I'll always remember Arnie Gunnlaugsson, the Iceman, scoring in each of the shoot-outs. He was brilliant, technically superb and very gifted. I think he was just a bit weak, mentally perhaps, especially in our team at that time which was full of huge characters. He was probably in the wrong side for the way that he played, as we were quite physical and direct. He didn't give us the energy we needed, as he wasn't the kind to chase and hassle, but he would have suited a more ball-playing team.

I would say, that along with Muzzy, he was probably up there as the best technical player in the squad at that time. He could really take a penalty too. His strikes were never in doubt. Muzzy scored the winning penalty against Leeds, knocking them out like he helped to do the year before. The Fulham game was something else though. We gifted them a 2-0 lead, with a poor backpass by Walshy, and we were minutes away from being knocked out, when Marshy grabbed us a lifeline, and then Walshy made up for his error with a thumping volley.

We always put balls into the box, absolutely bombarded sides, and that night Fulham didn't have the muscle to handle us. We were the never-say-die side. As I've said already, many times, we just didn't know when we were beaten. In extra time, Fulham went ahead through Chris Coleman, but again we took the aerial route and put so much pressure on them. Marshy was there again and got us level, before one of his trademark ridiculous celebrations.

Marshy always hit the target. If the ball was bouncing around the area, you'd put your house on him getting on the end of it and making the keeper work. I came close to winning it for us in injury time of extra time, but we went to penalties. Arnie stepped up first again and scored. As Tim was injured, Pegguy was in goal. He held the ball for a while to delay things and Coleman skied his penalty. Sav put us 2-0 up and then Paul Trollope missed his too. Graham [Fenton] came on as a late substitute and with his first kick he put us 3-0 up and then Geoff Horsfield's penalty was saved and we were in the semi-finals. We just had that knack for grinding out results when it mattered, which made us such a formidable cup side.

In the final of the three shoot-outs, Tim was back in goal to face Arsenal. He made some unbelievable saves that night, including point-blank stuff from Davor Suker. If you watch that game back, Tim and Sav are just throwing themselves in front of the ball.

By the time of the penalties, Pegguy was on for Tim, who was injured. Arnie and Sav scored theirs, before Lee Dixon's was saved. Fenton slotted, then Matty, before Stef Oakes's penalty was saved by David Seaman. Thierry Henry scored to take the tie to sudden death. Stuart Campbell then scored for us. He was the nominated taker at youth level and I never took penalties. When Patrick Vieira scored, I had to take one and I was so relieved to see it hit the net. Gilles Grimandi then saw his penalty saved and we had done it again. Watching this back made the hairs stand up on the back of my neck. I know that Martin would have loved us to go on and win the FA Cup, but circumstances went against us [losing to eventual winners Chelsea in the fifth round in 1997 and 2000]. Given that Leicester are yet to win it, that would have been special.

In the League Cup semi-final we went to Aston Villa for the first leg without Lenny, Muzzy and TC; the heart of the side. We held on for a 0-0 draw. After the game their boss, John Gregory said of us: 'It would be nice if they [Leicester] tried to cross the halfway line in the second leg.'

With the injuries we had, and players playing who weren't fully fit, plus the demands of all those extra-time games, replays and penalty shoot-outs, we were always going to find it tough to be at our best. Matty was walking pitchside after the draw at Villa Park and overheard Big Ron Atkinson in his punditry role referring to Leicester as 'square pegs in round holes' as Matty was having to play upfront.

In the second leg, we did cross the halfway line, John. It was Matty, playing upfront with me on this occasion, who held off Ugo Ehiogu, which was not easy to do, to guide the perfect header home to give us the lead. Matty was heading backwards, so it was very difficult for him to still be able to beat the goalkeeper from there. We held on to win 1-0 and reach Wembley again.

After the game, Matty saw Big Ron and shouted, 'Square pegs in round holes, hey Ron?' and walked off smiling, knowing that we were heading to Wembley. We were cup specialists. We knew how to stop teams from beating us, and knew how to get over the line. People may have said we were negative or lucky, but we just kept proving them wrong. I remember the fans around this time singing, 'Boring, boring, Leicester!' which we as players loved as it summed up our mentality.

I think whereas people had liked us when we first got promoted, they were now maybe a little bit jealous of our success, or maybe they'd just had enough of us? We didn't care a bit. We weren't always pretty, but then Martin didn't have the budget of other managers, but our achievements in those four and a half seasons under him were astonishing. We certainly weren't boring and the fans knew that. Look at how many late goals we scored, cup runs, trips to Wembley and penalty shoot-outs. They were amazing days. It's been so enjoyable watching the O'Neill years back for the purpose of writing this book. I'd forgotten just how good we were. We constantly punched above our weight and pissed people off, and we loved every minute of it. Filbert Street was bouncing and the players felt that bond with the fans throughout. We were unfashionable and we worked hard and they loved us for it. We were a working-class team playing for working-class people. Knocking Aston Villa out was a special night. They were the biggest club in the Midlands and yet we'd had the sign over them for a while. Growing up in Leicester, I'd seen us lose to Villa and Coventry over the years, but now we had their number and it was a great source of pride for everyone at the club.

* * *

The final was another special day. We faced Tranmere Rovers and in fairness to them, they did well, but we should have won by more. If you are offered a 2-1 win in a cup final though, you take it. Matty got both goals, was captain and won the man of the match award. It couldn't have gone much better for him. David Kelly equalised for them on the day and that gave us a real scare, but Gupps and Matty combined again to put us ahead late on. Matty was in such good form at that time, both as a defender and as a goalscorer. I actually went through on goal in the final, with the score at 1-0 and was fouled by Clint Hill who was sent off. We missed chances, but when the final whistle went we knew we had put right the wrongs of the previous year against Spurs, particularly for TC. He felt he'd missed his chance to win a major trophy, so it was extra special for him. Tranmere deserve so much credit for getting to the final and I suppose we ended their fairytale. For me, personally, having my family there again and so many of our fans, it is a memory I will never forget.

By the time of the final, it had started to get to the stage where I knew my time at Leicester was coming to an end. I think Spurs were interested in me, but my agent made it clear that Liverpool were keen. I knew they had been interested for years, but now it was real.

I don't think this has been made public until now, but I had a pre-contract agreement with Liverpool, stating that I could join them for £9m at the end of the season. Liverpool wanted me sooner as they were chasing the Champions League, so they paid £11m to get me in March. It was a strange time, but I felt like I'd done what I needed to do, by helping Leicester win the League Cup and that it was time to move on. We had qualified for Europe, so it seemed like a good time to take on another challenge.

Martin wasn't very happy with me. Jon Holmes, Gary Lineker's agent, was the man that signed me when I was young, and then I was passed on within the agency to Struan Marshall who became my agent. At a later date, Struan left the agency and as I knew him, I stayed with him. Jon, being a big Leicester fan, had told Martin O'Neill that I was going to sign a new contract with the club and everything would be fine. So when I decided to leave, which I was always going to do, Martin wasn't pleased with me. I hadn't changed my mind though. I did what I'd always intended to do. I was being fair to all parties. Leicester were prepared to offer the same contract that Liverpool did, but it was never about money. Muzzy and Lenny's terms were increased and I think Martin saw a future with us all together, pushing for the top six.

I spoke to Martin many years later and he admitted that my departure was the beginning of the end and obviously, just a few months later, he left too. Martin even had a go at me about it when I re-joined him at Aston Villa many years later. He never let things go, did Martin. I did reply by saying that he'd left soon after, but he wasn't having any of that. When I was in the process of leaving Leicester, I felt like people were talking about my potential and I wanted to realise that and show them that I could compete at the highest level. I supported Liverpool as a kid, but Leicester became my team as it was my home town and I'd come up through the ranks with them. Liverpool were the only team for me if I was going to leave, so once I knew they wanted me, I knew I had to take that plunge. I didn't want to sit at Leicester and be comfortable and I know it was the right decision. I looked back and I made four Wembley appearances in five years at Leicester and fans still speak about that team today, even though they've won the Premier League more recently.

My farewell game was at Filbert Street and we demolished Sunderland 5-2 and paraded the League Cup trophy for the fans. I couldn't have had a better goodbye. By this time, I was playing up front with Stan Collymore, who Martin had brought in, in typical Martin style, finding someone with talent who was unwanted or unloved and he got the best out of him.

Stan scored a hat-trick that day, I got one, along with two assists, and Stef Oakes got the fifth goal. That Sunderland

Stick your chest out. I was proud to play for my hometown club and loved my time in the centre of excellence and youth team.

My first goal at Filbert Street, against Norwich City in a 3-2 home win. I can still hear David Nish screaming at me to receive the ball from Simon Grayson. What a feeling.

All the support I needed.
I wouldn't leave my mum,
Albertine's side as a child,
and my dad, Tyrone, helped
to start my love of sport
and competing.

Que Sera, Sera, we're going to Wem-ber-ley! My cross for
Garry Parker's volley was enough to see off Stoke in the
1996 First Division play-off semi-finals.

Back in the big time! I'd had a taste of the Premier League, now I was going back there
for good. From left to right: Kevin Poole, me, Julian Watts, Colin Hill and Muzzy Izzet.

The gaffer and his skipper. What can I say about these two men? Martin O'Neill was a genius for Leicester and had a great influence on me. Steve Walsh was the ultimate warrior; brave as a lion, I looked up to him, as we all did and I'm proud to have him as a friend.

All smiles. Another new contract. There was always interest in me, but I knew Leicester was the right place for me to be in those early years. From left to right: Martin O'Neill, me and former chairman Tom Smeaton.

Flying Foxes. We weren't just making up the numbers. Here I am scoring our second goal against Manchester United in the League Cup fourth round in November 1996, on our way to the final.

Foxes Never Quit. We were dead and buried against Middlesbrough at Wembley in the 1997 League Cup Final, but with Walshy coming forward and Steve Claridge a constant menace, we were always a threat. That team never knew when they were beaten. My last-gasp tap-in set up a replay at Hillsborough.

We've done it! Neil Lennon lets me know just how happy he is that Leicester City are the 1997 League Cup winners, thanks to Steve Claridge's winner. Lenny was the heartbeat of that side, another incredible player and someone I would reunite with in later years.

Simon 'Larry' Grayson and I hold the trophy as thousands of Leicester fans line the streets of the city to celebrate. Larry always impressed me, especially the way he came back after a bit of stick from the fans to win two player of the year awards.

The scruffiest striker in town. But boy, could he play. Ian Marshall was lethal and I learned a lot from him. Atlético Madrid could only kick him off the pitch as he was unplayable that night.

I always wanted to play for England, so being called up to the squad and training with legends like Paul Ince, David Beckham and Paul Scholes, ahead of the Euro 2000 play-off first leg against Scotland was a dream for me.

My first start for the England senior team, against Argentina at Wembley in February 2000. I gave them the run-around and Sensini was substituted before half-time. I also nearly gave O'Neill kittens when I landed awkwardly on my back, days before Leicester returned to Wembley.

Matt's my boy! Big Matty Elliott heads home his second goal of the day to win the 2000 League Cup Final against Tranmere, both headers from Steve Guppy corners. Matt was a huge presence for us and a very good player too. Another incredible find by Martin O'Neill.

What might have been? I only played for a brief period with Stan Collymore, but we really hit it off; finishing with a 5-2 win over Sunderland, a hat-trick for him and a goal for me. Stan said I would thrive at Liverpool and I'd admired him since Mark McGhee told me to watch him. What a talent Stan was.

It was a dream for me to sign for Liverpool and I couldn't have wished to play for a better manager than Gerard Houllier. He was like a father figure to me and many others too and I'm still in touch with him today.

I was used to the glare of the media playing for Leicester and England, but joining Liverpool was intense. In hindsight, I wasn't quite ready for that leap, for leaving home and coping with my time off-field. I should have asked for help, but football was the saviour.

side was a decent outfit too, but we were on fire. It was a glimpse of the side we could have become under Martin. I spoke to Stan about Liverpool, as we roomed together for a while, and he said it would be a great move for me. He'd had that experience of playing at the top level for a big club and I craved that. I hadn't experienced that cauldron as I was loved at Leicester. I'd also remembered, as I've said, watching him play for Nottingham Forest when I was on the bench for Leicester and Mark McGhee made me focus on him. I felt like I could go and emulate him.

Unfortunately, Stan broke his ankle away at Derby County not long after the Sunderland game, and it started to unravel for Leicester. Stan was different. I roomed with him and he would keep himself to himself a lot of the time, but then he would spark into life and be the centre of attention. I think we would have complemented each other's games had we played together for longer. I celebrated my last goal for Leicester by running along, doing hi-fives with supporters, just as I did for the one I rocketed in off the bar in my Premier League home debut against Southampton.

While Martin may have been gutted to lose me, the club got the £11m, which was a record sale at the time and was a lot of money back in 2000. Once I'd left, as I'll talk about later, I wondered whether I'd made the right decision to leave. I had only known Leicester; it was easy for me, I was liked and I knew everyone and how everything worked. Liverpool was so alien to me. I was out of my comfort zone, but football always sorts that out. I knew that the more I played, the more settled I would feel.

I was so young when I left Leicester, and La Manga, that season, was a perfect example of that. Just before we played Tranmere in the League Cup final, the squad went to La Manga in Spain for a few days of warm weather training, which was always code for a booze up.

I was up in my room when it all kicked off and didn't know anything about what had happened. Apparently Gary Lineker was there at the same time as the squad, who were drinking heavily in the complex bar. Allegedly, Marshy was shouting 'Mr Fucking Match of the Day' at him, so Gary, rather wisely, soon left. One of the lads even had his pants around his ankles, while doing karaoke! Marshy rang Martin, who was still back in the UK and was set to fly out to join us all, asking him if we could stay out past the curfew.

Marshy was always cheeky, bless him. Stan allegedly let a fire extinguisher off and we were chucked out of the place and banned, around 24 hours after arriving. Martin was fuming. He spoke to John Robertson, ordered everyone home and absolutely destroyed us when we got back. Walshy was still drunk when we got home and I can remember him speaking up and I was thinking, 'This really isn't the time to do it, Wal.' All the headlines were 'Fireman Stan' and a lot of damage was done, but it was of the time. Those boys loved a drink and it was always a risk if we were away and letting our hair down. I think if we were ever on our own, away from Martin, there was always the risk of something happening. Even when the gaffer got off the coach after an away game, it was carnage and the coaching staff couldn't really handle us.

We didn't really train whenever we went away, either. It was always drinking, relaxing and often a bit of golf. Before the Aston Villa semi-final, we were sunning it up and drinking in Tenerife. I had a few, but I wasn't in the same league as the senior guys. In one training session out there, with everyone either pissed or halfway there, one of the lads just stood and pissed their pants, urine running down their leg, while the coach Steve Walford gave instructions. You'd never have believed we were professional footballers. It was like an 18–30s trip!

Those trips were always just team bonding; to get away from everything and to have a good time together. It worked. We'd have a great time, forget about everything and then come back ready to play. You wouldn't get away with it now. We all socialised together; we'd go to Baffone [now Altro Mondo], an Italian restaurant in Leicester, tucked away from the main streets, and then go on and drink together in other places. I doubt many teams do that now. A lot of us lived in Leicester and we were really good friends. Players are more professional in their preparation now and they spend time with their families at home, which I understand completely, but we had such a laugh back then.

Leicestershire is a beautiful place to live and I get why so many of that team settled in the area and still live there today. Leicester means a lot to me and whenever I go home, it is special. By the time I left, I had bought a new house, but I hardly lived there as my move to Liverpool happened soon after. I eventually sold my place, so I don't really have any memories of it. The house was near to the Oadby Racecourse, just over the road from it, not too far from where I'd grown up in Evington. Life was changing pretty fast for me. I had grown up in Leicester, from a boy to a man, but moving to Liverpool was going to require another level of maturity from me. I was about to step into another world.

CHAPTER SIX

All Alone, Surrounded by Trophies

I WAS more excited than nervous about joining Liverpool. I could have gone elsewhere, but it had to be Liverpool. Doug Ellis, may he rest in peace, the former Aston Villa chairman, was badgering Peter Taylor, the former England under-21 manager, to get him in a room with me while I was on national team duty, as he wanted to speak to me, but nothing was going to stop me from signing for Liverpool. Once you know a club you support wants you, the rest is just noise.

I knew what I could bring to Liverpool. I had played for England at all youth levels by this stage and I was in the senior side. I'd won trophies with Leicester, played four seasons of Premier League football and I'd scored against Liverpool. I believed I could make that jump. Nothing ever fazed me on the football field. What did faze me was the thought of leaving home and moving away from the comfort of Leicester, to the unknown of Liverpool.

The thought of walking out at the magnificent Anfield, hearing 'You'll Never Walk Alone' being sung by everyone, was something I couldn't wait to experience. Training would be fine too. These places were my arenas, my chance to express myself. It doesn't matter what's going on in your life away from the game, once you step out on to the training field, or the stadium pitch, you forget everything else. All your troubles and worries just drift away. But what was I going to do with the rest of my time? That's why it's so difficult for former footballers to cope; those with difficulties don't have the release of the game anymore. If they don't become a coach, or stay in the game in some capacity, they can't replace the sheer joy of playing the game they love.

Looking back, I understand why I felt the way I did, being apprehensive about moving away, but now it just seems silly, almost trivial. It was 2000; there were no satellite navigation systems, no Google Maps, the internet was in its infancy. I didn't know where I was going and I felt lost. The simplest of things would bring me down. In Leicester, I would finish training and I had my mates around the corner from me. I could just go and chill with them. I could even go to their workplace and chat to them. At Liverpool, I didn't even know how to get to the training ground. Our player liaison officer, Norman Gard, who was brilliant, had too many people to take care of. We had foreign players who didn't speak English very well, so he couldn't be expected to spend all of his time with me and I wouldn't have wanted him to. They needed their whole life organising; house, mortgage, bank account, all the forms you need, they needed help with them all. When I first moved up there, I was in a really nice hotel in Woolton, quite a family-oriented place. Then I moved into an apartment over the road, before I eventually bought my house.

I can remember going in to training, loving playing alongside my team-mates and being really happy with my football life. I'd have lunch at the training ground but then come home, walk in through my door and just lay down on the floor, staring at the ceiling. I was just motionless, looking up and wondering whether I had made the right decision. I would cry my eyes out. I don't think I was depressed, it didn't feel like I was anyway. It was nothing to do with football. I was isolated. I missed my friends and my family, my home comforts. I missed Leicester as everything was so easy there. In the middle of the day, I'd have no one to speak to. I was so lonely. My friends and family were at work, getting on with their lives. Not many people had mobile phones. It would be 2.30pm and I was just all alone.

I was 22 years old, but a young 22, despite the fact that I had two children by then. I had to grow up very quickly. It seems strange to look back and remember how poorly I coped with the change in my life, but I guess it was because I didn't really let anyone know. I didn't ask for help. I don't think it was the done thing to ask back then. I love that my kids can speak out now; they can ask family, friends, coaches and teachers for help. Back then, in my culture and in society as a whole, I had to keep these issues to myself and learn how to deal with them. People will probably laugh when they read this, but I was mature in football terms by the age of 16, but at 22 I was still just a kid when it came to off-the-field stuff.

I didn't want to be a burden to anyone. I didn't ask my team-mates to show me around Liverpool or anything like that. I wouldn't have dared go out for a meal in those early times. I'd just get some microwave meals in, probably the worst thing I could have done too in terms of nutrition and health. I watched a BET Comedy Central boxset and would piss myself laughing. That was my escape from my new life. Another thing that bothered me was that I didn't find a proper barber straightaway. For a black person, with textured hair, you can't just walk in off the street to any hairdresser. It was probably 18 months before I found a place to go to. During that time, I was driving back to Leicester to get my hair cut at my old barbers, or I was trying out this Greek place in Liverpool, but you know the difference. My hair looked awful.

Finally, I found a place which was just around the corner from where I lived. Unfortunately, not long after, the barber, who was from Trinidad, was deported for fighting. I discovered other barbers nearby, so the saga of my hair was resolved. Nowadays, you just type things in to your smartphone and you know where and when you can get stuff. Back then, I was just struggling through.

I started to walk around town a little bit, but I would stay away from areas of the city that were busy. I knew I was going to get recognised as I was playing for England and Liverpool, and I was the club's record signing at the time. I was uncomfortable with my surroundings, so I would just put a hat on, get my head down and go and do what I needed to do and get back home as soon as I could.

I knew a lot of the players already from my time with England: Robbie Fowler, Jamie Redknapp and Michael Owen; I'd played alongside Jamie Carragher since the age of 16, and then, of course, Steven Gerrard. They and the rest of the squad took to me well. Everyone was very friendly. Training was a bit strange and took some getting used to though. It was full-on and hugely different to Leicester. In the week, apart from the old versus young games at Leicester, you weren't really encouraged to tackle, in order to avoid injuries. It was half-paced, save it for the weekend, that kind of thing.

I can remember training on the Friday before my debut on the Saturday for Liverpool and I received the ball into my feet with my back to goal, and Stéphane Henchoz went sliding right through me and cleaned me out. Welcome to Liverpool, Emile. I got up, and then I realised you could do that as no one reacted. I thought, 'Okay, that's how it's going to be here.' We would train how we would play. I liked that. I wanted to have a go, to be myself, to express myself and not hold back.

On my debut, against Sunderland at Anfield, I won the penalty for us in the first few minutes, which Patrik Berger scored and we drew 1-1. Kevin Phillips equalised, also from the spot, and he was on fire that season. Playing against Sunderland was strange in itself, as I'd obviously played against them a week earlier, winning 5-2 with Leicester. Michael Owen came up to me after the game and said, 'See, if I'd have been playing you'd have got me a goal already.' I think it was his way of letting me know I was going to be valued by him and the club. It was nice to get in front of the fans finally, after a lot of talk and anticipation.

People ask me whether I felt the pressure of playing for Liverpool and the weight of the £11m fee. Initially I didn't. I honestly didn't. I couldn't control what the media said, what Gerard Houllier was willing to pay for me, and I didn't care about transfer fees or about opinions of others. I just wanted to get out there and play football. Look at the fee Manchester United paid for Paul Pogba. It's hammered home every single time he is discussed as a player. Eventually, it seeps into your mind and you do start to question yourself. I'm not saying he does, but I did. I'd forgotten about the fee, but if you are reminded of it every time you are interviewed, it's eventually going to get into your head. If you tell a kid they can't do something, over time they are going to believe you and then repeat that they can't do it.

I felt like I settled in okay. People are always going to judge you by goals as a striker. I got three in my first 12 games at the end of the 1999/00 season, but things didn't end well for the team. I'd signed earlier to chase a Champions League place, and I'd come in to help push us over the line. Having won five on the bounce, we failed to win any of our final five league games, including a 2-0 home defeat against Leicester. I was frustrated as I wanted to show my old club that I'd moved on to something bigger and better. We played fine that night, but nothing went right for us. Paddy Berger hit the crossbar and he could really hit them. My mate, Pegguy Arphexad, was in goal for Leicester and he only saw the ball when it came back off the bar. It was that much of a rocket.

The season ended at Bradford City, who made their infamous great escape by beating us 1-0, costing us a place in the Champions League in the process. They had a crazy pitch invasion at Bradford and Stéphane Henchoz was struck by a fan. There were thousands running at us and when it's like that you just have to get yourself off the field as quickly as possible.

We could never have known the path that defeat would lead us down.

In the summer of 2000, Houllier brought in Gary McAllister, Pegguy Arphexad, Nick Barmby, Christian Ziege and Markus Babbel. Gary was like a father figure. We had a fairly young group of lads at that stage, so Macca coming in was great as he was someone with wisdom and understanding, who you could confide in. He was 35 when he joined Liverpool and many questioned why we were signing him, but the influence he had on Steven Gerrard, and the performances he put in for the club, answered any doubters. He was a special guy to have alongside us.

Patrice Bergues, Houllier's assistant, was Pegguy's coach as a youth player, so that's the connection there. As I've said about Pegguy already, he was a hugely positive character and more than capable of being a number one, let alone a reserve goalkeeper. It was great to have him and his family around again. I lived near him for a while before I moved, but culturally, it was important for me to have him around me. We don't often talk about that kind of thing in life, but I grew up in a certain culture and Pegguy understood that so it made a real difference having him with me.

Markus was a huge name. Watching how he worked and his dedication to the game was inspiring. He was sturdy, solid, a quality right-back. He was very professional. I'm not talking about Markus here, but we as English players get labelled a certain way, and Germans are always classed as professional. Many Germans that I've played with, or known, would be on the beer every day. They drink every day as it's part of their culture, whereas we binge drink. We look at beer as something you can't have unless it's after a certain time, but they and many Europeans, have alcohol as part of their daily life, as a normal beverage to have in the day to relax. Just like having a tea or coffee. Italian footballers will have a glass of wine the night before a game. I've always thought our attitude was a little strange on this subject. Ziege was pretty much the same as Markus; as efficient as they come and another great name to bring in to the squad.

Nick Barmby was a strange signing, one that stood out given that we took him from the blue half of Merseyside. In a similar way to Markus, he gave us exactly what we needed. He was a very intelligent player, who made some incredible runs and scored memorable goals. Moving from Everton to Liverpool though? That must have been very tough for Nick to deal with. He must have had balls of steel to cope with the pressure of that.

Later in the season, we added Igor Biscan and Jari Litmanen to the squad. Igor found it difficult. He joined with a reputation as one of the best young players in Croatia. I think he experienced some loneliness, in the same way that I did when I first signed for Liverpool. He had no one around him and was in an alien country. He was quiet, but I got on well with him. His English improved during his time at the club. I can remember him flying his mates over and they would bring him things, home comforts, Croatian food to help him. I don't think we were ever sure what Igor's best position was, which probably didn't help him either. I liked him in midfield, but we played him everywhere.

Igor loved the gym. I was injured once, and at Melwood, where the gym was situated, there's a glass window backing on to the physio room. It meant staff could keep an eye on people in the gym. There would normally be someone in there with you, but Igor was on his own and decided to do maximum weights on his chest. If you are going to do that, you should always have someone there to supervise you. He pushed the weights up, and then when they came down the bar was pushing down on his throat. He couldn't move and was trying to scream for help. No one could hear him though. Luckily, a member of staff was walking past, saw Igor through the glass and rushed in to help release him. From where I was being treated, I couldn't have seen him as he wasn't in my eye line. It could have been much worse for him though.

Adding Jari to our group was really special for me. He's a legend of the game. I was so excited to meet him and see what he was like. Jari was an ultra-professional character. I had watched him play for Barcelona, for Finland and Ajax. His touch was perfect. You couldn't really get close to him on the training pitch, as he knew where everyone was around him. That awareness was a gift he had. It was a real privilege to play alongside him. As soon as I saw the ball go into his feet, I'd start running as I knew he'd find me with a through-ball. One game, I think it was Manchester City at home, the ball came into him and we didn't even look at each other, he just put me in over the top and I scored. He was so talented.

I realised after joining Liverpool that I had to adapt from the role I'd played at Leicester, which was more about holding the ball up, winning free kicks and giving the defence and midfield some breathing space. I was looked upon to create a spark for us. I now had to change because we had more of the ball. At Liverpool, with all due respect to Leicester, there was a whole team of names and people who could do something creative. I had to focus on where I made my runs, how I linked up with team-mates, rather than generally making myself busy at Leicester. The ball also came to me a lot more directly at Leicester, but at Liverpool it would come through midfield; apart from in European away games, where goalkeeper Sander Westerveld would kick directly to my chest and we would start the move from there, which was an effective tactic to get us forward quickly.

I don't know where to start with the 2000/01 season. For so many reasons, for the trophies, the goals and the adventure we went on and the memories we created, it has to be the best season in my playing career. In the League Cup, we beat Chelsea, Stoke, Fulham after extra time, and then faced Crystal Palace over two legs in the semi-final. We lost 2-1 in the away leg and their striker Clinton Morrison spoke to the media after the game and said, 'The form I'm in, I think I'd have put away the chances that Michael Owen and Emile Heskey missed.' The papers went big on the quote and said that Clinton was going to teach Michael how to score goals. You don't teach Michael how to do what he does best.

In the second leg we won 5-0 and poor Clinton did a complete air shot in front of the Kop. As the story goes, apparently Gary McAllister went over to him and said, 'Don't worry lad, Michael Owen would have scored that!' That whole incident was an example of how the media can run with something and take advantage of what a young lad has said. It was probably tongue-in-cheek given he'd done so well in the first leg, but he learned a lesson that night. It's slightly different now as players own the narrative a lot more with social media and club media being more prominent, but back then, if you said the wrong thing to the wrong journalist, you would soon know about it.

The final was held at the Millennium Stadium, Cardiff, while Wembley was being rebuilt, against Birmingham City. I played in all of our finals that season. I was up front alongside Robbie Fowler and we were doing well, popping the ball around with pace and purpose. I flicked on a ball to Robbie, he let it bounce and did what he does, scoring a superb goal to put us 1-0 up with 30 minutes on the clock. I had a good relationship with Robbie. He was a good captain which is perhaps forgotten sometimes. He was very good at keeping everyone together.

Vladimir Smicer had a chance to put us 2-0 up, but Darren Purse equalised with a late penalty and after a goalless extra time, we went to penalties. I didn't take one, but we squeezed past them 5-4 and I had a hold on my first trophy as a Liverpool player. A lot of people didn't value the League Cup back then, perhaps they still don't now, but I did. It's a trophy, a final, and a day out for the fans and a route into European football. I experienced that with Leicester and people still speak about those days now. It's also unique as it's a cup that you win during the season, as opposed to it being at the end, so you can use that positive feeling to inspire the rest of your season and create that winning habit.

The FA Cup run was great. I scored twice against Rotherham United in round three and came on as a substitute against Wycombe in the semi-final at Villa Park and scored with just over ten minutes to go. It was a header on a rainy day in the Midlands and I used the wet turf to go sliding, face first, towards the Liverpool fans to celebrate. Robbie made it 2-0 soon after and then Wycombe got one back to give us a scare, but we were heading back to Cardiff again. This time it was Arsenal. In fairness, I think we were battered that day. It was a real smash and grab game, known as the 'Michael Owen Final'.

Thierry Henry rounded Sander Westerveld and saw his shot handled on the line at the near post by Stéphane Henchoz. Thierry was furious yet the referee, Steve Dunn, just didn't see it. Freddie Ljungberg then put Arsenal 1-0 up with less than a quarter of the game to go and we were struggling to turn things around. Perhaps the volume of matches had finally got to us all?

Michael was still sharp enough to pounce in the box and acrobatically turn the ball past David Seaman to equalise, with just seven minutes to go. The stadium was expecting extra time, but not Michael. With 88 minutes on the clock, Patrik Berger picked the ball up a little outside our penalty area, shifted it on to his left foot and played a long, accurate ball for Michael to run on to. He had Lee Dixon and Tony

Adams either side of him, but he outpaced them both and then from a tight angle, shot with his left foot across David Seaman and just inside the far post. If you're a Liverpool fan, if you're a fan of football from that era, you won't need me to describe it. You'll already be able to picture it. He was out of this world in those final minutes. We had gone from losing a final we'd underperformed in, to stealing it in the most dramatic of ways. It's a day I'll never forget.

We had the knack that season. We knew how to see a game out. Okay, we didn't win the league, but in the cups we didn't just believe we could beat anyone; we went out there and proved it in three competitions. In Europe that season, we would be structured, compact and would get a result. When we brought teams back to Anfield, they weren't beating us, no way. There was an air of invincibility about us.

In the UEFA Cup we knocked out Rapid Bucharest, Slovan Liberec, Olympiacos, Roma, Porto and Barcelona. It was so demanding, and these were good, experienced sides. It wasn't an easy run, but at no point did we doubt ourselves. Houllier instilled that belief in us and the players went out there and delivered on his game plan each and every time.

The UEFA Cup final was something else. I know that everyone remembers it, given the 5-4 scoreline, but I can't remember the game at all! That's right, I played in the game and honestly, I can't remember a thing. I was exhausted and I was genuinely just playing on autopilot by then. I was mentally fucked.

I started this game, as I did in the other two finals too, but I've had to watch the game back for the purpose of writing this book. There are moments there that felt as if I was seeing them for the very first time. As footballers, that can happen sometimes. You are bouncing from one game to the next, hotel to stadium, training ground to home, airport to another city in another country. It can feel like the film *Groundhog Day*, where each day is the same and eventually you just need a break, just to recharge your batteries.

Instead, here I was playing in a UEFA Cup final! It was an incredible, end-to-end game. We were 2-0 up, then 3-1 up and in control, but Alaves weren't in the final by luck. They had Javi Moreno, who pulled them back to 3-3, and Jordi Cruyff, and they had spirit. It was a real test for us. A lesser team would have laid down and let the momentum continue in their favour. Moreno's second goal was one of those I hate. He shot under our defensive wall as we jumped. I don't agree with jumping in a defensive wall, and he was crafty and banked on us doing that.

I then came off and Robbie, who replaced me, put us 4-3 up, before Cruyff equalised to make it 4-4 in the 89th minute. Alaves had two players sent off in extra time and with just three minutes to go, an own goal by Delfi Geli, from a McAllister free kick, was enough to win it for us under the golden goal rule; an exhausting, remarkable night for everyone. We had completed a unique treble of cup victories. The final was played in the Westfalenstadion, in Dortmund, and our supporters just swamped the city and the stadium. What I do remember of the night, the picture I see in my mind when I think back to it, is of all those thousands of Liverpool fans, singing and celebrating. That's something I could simply never forget.

It was just the consistency that we were lacking; it's what cost us winning the league. We could beat anyone; we could win big, high-pressure games but we couldn't do it week in, week out in the Premier League. I'm not making excuses, but maybe the volume of cup games had an effect as well. However, Manchester United did their treble in 1999 and they handled the fixtures. I believe we were capable of more success, but there's a difference between saying it and actually turning that into a league title.

I made 62 appearances that season, including England games, and scored 23 goals. That included my first goal in European football, against Slovan Liberec; my first Merseyside derby goals, home and away; one against my old club, Leicester, and one against Wycombe Wanderers in the FA Cup semi-final. Only Michael scored more for Liverpool than me that season.

The 2001/02 season followed; Gerard strengthened by bringing in John-Arne Riise, an absolute fitness fanatic. What struck me with him was that everyone hurts in pre-season and no one likes it. Only John did. He loved the running and he hated to lose. Paddy Berger was really good at running and he would catch John up and that would push him to run even faster. I didn't know he had anything else in him but he'd sprint away. I would be standing there, shaking my head. I just didn't get it and I was competitive and could run distances, but I didn't know why he wanted to run to that level. Milan Baros came in too and he was great. He was a strong runner with the ball. Sadly for me, he would take away some of my game time, but I didn't begrudge him that as he was a quality player and a good guy. It's a team game after all, and as long as I could play my part, I was happy.

Chris Kirkland was a very talented goalkeeper, who found it difficult after a few injuries early on. He was very unlucky. I think he was tarnished with being injury-prone by the media, but if you look at his career, he still played a lot of games. Jerzy Dudek, another goalkeeper, was signed at the same time, with the aim of them both competing and pushing each other for the number one jersey. That signalled the end for Sander at Liverpool, unfortunately, and he left at the end of the year. I thought Sander did well for us. He had a great kick on him, as did Chris and Jerzy. I know that Sander was under pressure and that the media had picked out some of his errors, but on the whole I felt like he did a great job for us. Goalkeeping errors are always going to stand out more, given where they play on the pitch and that the error will often lead directly to a goal, but he can be proud of how he played for us. Jerzy overcame some early issues as well, which also showed his strength of character.

We also added Nicolas Anelka on loan, who Gerard knew from his time with the French national academy at

Clairefontaine. I was so excited to play alongside him. He was a similar age to me and I'd played against him for England under-18s. I didn't feel that Nic got the respect he should have been given during his career, especially in England. Those who criticised him just didn't know him well enough. He was quiet. He was called 'Le Sulk', but he wasn't like that at all, at least not in my dealings with him. I was quiet too. I understood where he was coming from. He was branded that way because he was French, which was hugely unfair. Once I'd approached him, he would talk and we had some nice conversations, with a little bit of banter as well. I couldn't understand what people were saying about him. I know he had some issues with agents, but that's external stuff, the people around him. That's not him, so what people were saying about his character was wrong in my opinion. I loved the way he played, and me, him and Michael struck up a good partnership.

There was lots of competition, with Milan as well. Robbie left around this time. That was sad as he was Mr Liverpool. He helped to make my time with the club more enjoyable and more successful of course. It hurt the fans a lot, I know, as he is an absolute legend in their eyes and rightly so. Abel Xavier joined as well. I didn't really know much about him, but he was reliable and was another solid addition.

As well as Robbie and Sander, Christian Ziege, Gary McAllister and Jamie Redknapp departed. I felt for Jamie. He had injury problems and didn't really play that much. He was the club captain, so was always present, but probably felt on the edge of it all in many ways. Having him around was great though; he was a leader, someone who helped to keep everyone positive and brought us all together. He was one of the last of the players from the 1990s and made way for Jamie Carragher and Steven Gerrard to take over the leadership of the team and squad.

We kicked off the 2001/02 season by winning two more trophies. We beat Manchester United 2-1 in the Charity Shield and then Bayern Munich 3-2 in the UEFA Super Cup. I didn't feel like Bayern knew about our directness, particularly in the way we would get the ball quickly up to Michael and me. We both scored in that game after Riise had put us ahead. We were 3-0 up and I think we surprised them a little. That showed the strength we had and the momentum we had gained by then. We were such a confident side, but to rip apart a side like Bayern Munich in a cup final was pretty special.

I can't speak highly enough of Gerard Houllier. I still speak to him today, which says a lot, and I know I'm not the only one. The influence he had, and continues to have on me, makes him one of the truly special people I have had the pleasure of working with. We had a great relationship. Right from the first meeting I thought he was a nice guy, friendly and understanding of people. I always remember him looking into my eyes, intensely, to check whether he felt I was getting enough sleep. He cared about absolutely everything and he was such a father figure to me and to many other players he worked with.

If I ever needed anything, I felt like he would be there for me. I just had to ask, which obviously I didn't always do. He would put his arm around me and he was perfect for my personality. Sometimes, I just needed that reassurance and encouragement. I was a quiet lad and, if I'm honest, I'm still a quiet lad now. Gerard was different to Martin O'Neill, but Martin could have that soft side, it was just that he didn't mind being ruthless if he needed to be. Gerard was never like that. He had Phil Thompson to do all the shouting and gesturing for him. I felt that Phil could go over the top at times, but I guess you can easily get caught up in the emotions of football. Gerard would have to pull him back at times, but Phil was definitely the bad cop of the partnership. It must have been weird for foreign lads trying to understand his anger, let alone his accent. I took Phil with a pinch of salt to be honest. He was there to motivate and shout. He didn't do a great deal of coaching, but when he did, he was working with the defence, so I didn't have as much contact with him. He was a strong voice though, and you could see what the club meant to him.

It was a huge shock when Gerard had his heart issues. I had pulled my hamstring in the Leeds game, and at half-time I was sitting in the physio room. It was down the corridor from the dressing room and I was waiting to be treated. Gerard came in and told the doctor, Mark Waller, that he didn't feel too well and was suffering from chest pains. I looked at Gerard and could see there was something wrong. I got up to ask him to sit down and he was telling me to stay where I was, to not make my injury any worse. I'm telling him to sit down as I'm worried about him.

We got him into a chair and the medical guys called for an ambulance immediately. Our physio, Dave Galley, treated Gerard initially. I moved out of the room as I could see it was serious and that I would just be getting in the way. He had professionals around him so there was nothing I would be able to do. I was one of a few people to be there, as the rest of the lads were in the dressing room preparing for the second half. If they'd have waited any longer, or if this had happened somewhere else, I hate to think what could have happened.

Jari replaced me for the second half and the lads went out to earn a 1-1 draw without knowing the extent of what had happened. Gerard had suffered a heart attack and only the subs on the day and myself would have known. He was popular with everyone, so it was a real shock to all of us and the mood was very sombre afterwards. Thankfully, Gerard was treated at the Royal Liverpool University Hospital and recovered from the incident. The levels of stress that football managers are under is, at times, off the chart. Gerard was a healthy man, but the stress must have taken its toll on him. Look at managers now. When they join a club they look smart, fresh, full of positive energy. Six months later, they are grey, tired and as if they have the weight of the world on their shoulders.

* * *

It was still a big season for us. We had Champions League football to contend with and got past Borussia Dortmund, Dynamo Kiev and Boavista, before a second group stage against Galatasaray, Roma and Barcelona. We then lost in the quarter-finals to eventual finalists, Bayer Leverkusen. They had Michael Ballack and he was at the peak of his career at that time. We bowed out 4-3 on aggregate and were disappointed as we'd become accustomed to winning everything. In my mind, we were going to go all the way and win the Champions League. We wanted to do it for Gerard, but we believed we could do it for ourselves. I never doubted us, but it was just one step too far. It was another gruelling season as I made 57 appearances, scoring 14 goals and we finished as runners-up in the Premier League, seven points behind Arsenal, and above Manchester United. It was our best finish during my time at the club, but in fairness, Arsenal were very worthy winners and were an incredible side.

When Phil became manager, during Gerard's five months of recovery, he had to change his methods. He mellowed a little and took on a lot of Gerard's traits. He didn't just shout at us, he was encouraging and showed a more fatherly side to his character. Perhaps that showed that he was playing a role as Gerard's assistant, offering that balance to his own character? Phil was more controlled during his time in charge and I felt he did very well in the role. It must have been tough for him to see how poorly Gerard was, and then have to step into his shoes, but he did the club proud in that period.

I wasn't happy that we didn't follow up the previous season with more notable success. Sure, the Charity Shield and the UEFA Super Cup are trophies and the quarter-finals of the Champions League is a decent showing, but I was craving more success after our treble. We all were. I wanted big trophies. At Liverpool, you are always judged by whether you can win the title. We didn't, and I'll always wish we did, to have been the group of guys that brought the title home to those amazing supporters, but it wasn't to be.

We had our own success and I'm sure we created lots of joy for everyone in the process. I wanted that success for people like Steven Gerrard and Jamie Carragher as well, for whom the club meant everything. When I joined, Stevie was a young lad and I had seen bits and pieces of his talent. Until you train regularly with someone like him, you don't realise just how good he is. For example, everyone thinks of Michael Owen and his pace. Stevie was quicker. Michael was quicker over ten yards, but once you go past that, Stevie would be faster. Now someone with that pace, strength, passing ability, box-to-box energy, timing, shooting and sheer will and determination, along with his leadership qualities, there's only one way they are going to go, and that's right to the top of the game. It didn't take a genius to see that as soon as you watched him play. He was always going to be the captain. We had Sami

Hyypia and Jamie, of course, but Stevie was eventually going to be the one. During my time at the club, he was developing and getting better with each passing season, before he became the world star he was for many years. Stevie and Paul Scholes would have to be the best two midfielders I played alongside. They were as close to perfection as you can get. They were truly world class.

CHAPTER SEVEN

Time to Say Goodbye

WE kicked off the 2002/03 season by losing 1-0 to Arsenal in the Community Shield, but the summer was probably more notable for our new signing; the controversial El Hadji Diouf. At the time, no one could understand why we had signed him. He had a great World Cup with Senegal, but we had been in talks with Nicolas Anelka, who had done well with us during his loan spell. He was a phenomenal player and his character, as I've said already, was fine. Despite this, we knew that Dioufy was a quality player and his stock was on the rise after the World Cup, so we were excited to have this talent join the squad.

Senegal were inspiring, reaching the quarter-finals of the World Cup, having beaten the holders, France, in the opening game. We also brought Salif Diao in, and Gerard signed both of these players before the World Cup, so he was sure what they could bring to Liverpool. Gerard wasn't the kind of manager who would sign a player based on a tournament, or a handful of decent performances. He was thorough and would base his judgement over a number of months or even years.

I felt like Dioufy was going to provide competition for me, another striker to battle for a place in the side. It turned out that he was shunted around a little, playing out on both wings, as a forward, and as a creative player, but not necessarily as an out-and-out striker. I want to put this down on paper right now; El Hadji had so much ability, he was absolute quality, but that was never really spoken about in this country due to the controversy that came with him. He was the kind of guy that craved being in the limelight. He wanted to be the centre of attention. If I was one-on-one with him, we could have a great conversation, but when he was in a group situation, he became loud, sociable, an extroverted character. He was confident, but then most footballers are; they have the talent, the money, the fame and the lifestyle that goes with it.

Dioufy wanted to be known by everyone. A lot of people would switch it on and off. As I've said, I was very shy as a kid and I'm still a reserved person now, so once I stepped off the pitch or the training ground, I went back to being normal. Dioufy just kept on bringing the noise to his life. That was his style. Not many people were able to get close to him, to get to know the real him. The thing is, I don't think he minded the controversy or the publicity. I think that was part of what he wanted. I don't know for sure, and you'd have to ask him, but I feel like the publicity helped with his notoriety and he played up to the role. If he was on the back page, the front page, any page, it didn't matter to him. That was the total opposite to me. I wanted my football to be the reason I was known and the rest, well, that was my private life and nothing to do with anyone else.

We started that season really well, with 30 points from the first 12 games and there was real excitement that we could finally deliver the title. We were top of the Premier League but then went 11 league games without a win. Our season fell away as quickly as it had got going. We were knocked out of the Champions League, in a group that contained Basel, Spartak Moscow and Valencia, which was hugely disappointing. Finishing third in the group dropped us into the UEFA Cup and we beat Vitesse Arnhem and then Auxerre, to set up a quarter-final tie with Celtic, and my old manager from Leicester, Martin O'Neill, and former colleagues Neil Lennon and Steve Guppy.

The first leg was away and our thinking was always to be sturdy, solid, and to try to nick a goal, but if you don't then don't lose the game. I scored and we came away with a 1-1 draw. It was tough. The noise, the hate. It was like nothing I had heard before. I caught up with Steve Walford and Martin afterwards, and that was nice. On the way back home, I was convinced that we were going to spank them back at Anfield. We'd done the hard part, now they were coming to our place and we were going to rip them apart.

Instead, we were battered. They played us off the park and beat us 2-0. We all expected to win. Perhaps we thought we'd already won the game? I don't know. We felt we could win the trophy, let alone the tie and maybe we were looking too far ahead. We were complacent and they were a solid side, full of big, strong guys, who could play a bit too. Martin got their game plan spot on, something I'd experienced so many times with Leicester; being the underdog, competing for every ball, making the most of set pieces and silencing the home crowd. He was a master at it. Celtic went on to reach the final and were unlucky to lose to Jose Mourinho's FC Porto, 3-2.

We didn't finish the season empty-handed though. We won the League Cup, beating Manchester United 2-0. It was becoming a bit of a thing for me, the League Cup. No wonder I get hired by them for promotional work now; six cup finals and four wins. It was a competition I always respected and loved our successes. At the time of writing, Ian Rush and I hold the record for the most final appearances, although he won five of them. That's something I am proud of. I suppose some of the Manchester City players will now catch us up.

On the way to the final, we beat Southampton, then Ipswich Town on penalties, beat Aston Villa in a dramatic game 4-3, and then Sheffield United in the semi-finals over two legs, before United in the final. It doesn't matter what competition you are playing in, United versus Liverpool is always a big deal.

It was another big season for me, where I played my part as well; 51 appearances and ten goals. I was still a big part of the team and I felt as if I was part of the future plans. You don't play that many games if the manager doesn't want you, put it that way. We finished fifth in the Premier League and qualified for the UEFA Cup. It may have felt like a disappointment to everyone, but we were competitive and we had another trophy in the cabinet. With football, sometimes it can be more a case, particularly nowadays, of how you are perceived rather than what you actually win. A manager can be judged by their style of play, their mood in press conferences, or the net spend of their transfers, rather than the games they win, the cup finals and the trophies they secure. That's wrong. If you are a winner, then you are delivering on the club's aims. Yes, there needs to be some style, some warmth to come with it, but that shouldn't be the main factor in judging success.

In November of that season, Leicester City were in real financial trouble. When I first realised what was happening at the club, I felt sick. It wasn't nice. I heard about the consortium being put together by Gary Lineker and his agent, Jon Holmes, and I contacted my financial advisors and my agent to say I wanted to help and be involved. In my mind, I was thinking there would be no Leicester City. I couldn't allow that. In reality, that wouldn't have been allowed to happen, but I wasn't to know that.

Leicester helped to make me the person I am today, they looked after me. If there was no Leicester, then there was no me. I felt that it was the right thing to do, and that if I donated some money to the consortium, it might encourage others to follow. I had a special affinity with the club. They allowed me to train there as a nine-year-old, to be nurtured and to then put me on a platform which took me to cup finals, to Liverpool, to England, to World Cups, to live out my dreams. How could I not give them something back to help them when they most needed it? I owed a lot to them.

It wasn't £100,000, it wasn't £150,000 that I put in, as is often documented, but it was a substantial amount. It helped, but it was so sad to see Leicester in that state. We'd enjoyed such a great run under Martin O'Neill and within two and a half years of me and him leaving, the club was on its knees. Back then, we had been begging for a new stadium. Don't get me wrong, there will only ever be one Filbert Street, but with the stadium the club moved into, Martin could have achieved even more and attracted better quality players to the club. Now they had the stadium, but the club was falling apart from the inside. I was proud to help them, but sad that they needed me to do it.

After I gave the club the money, I would receive financial reports, but I didn't have anything to do with the running of the club. I was a footballer; I didn't have the desire to know more about that side of things. My financial advisors would keep me updated with how the club was progressing; I just wanted to know that Leicester had a future, nothing else. When you look how the club has progressed over the years, it's great to see, but it's easy to forget how perilous things got. I was 24 when I invested. How many people can say that? I know you've got your club in Miami now, Becks, but did you have a stake in Leicester City in your twenties, like me? No, you did not, mate!

In the summer of 2003, the beginning of my final season at Liverpool, we brought in four notable signings: Steve Finnan, Harry Kewell, Anthony Le Tallec and Florent Sinama Pongolle.

Le Tallec and Pongolle were incredibly talented young players. They'd had great success at youth level, having played for Le Havre in France, and Gerard was very impressed with them. Expectation was high and this is where, as clubs, and not just Liverpool, I'm not convinced we do enough to help young overseas players.

We bring them in and throw them in at the deep end on the pitch. They can swim and float for a while, but if we don't support them off the field with their lifestyles, then they eventually sink on the field. We don't help people to adapt to the culture of our country and of our football.

These two lads would do things, normal things to them, like walking with a swagger, or rolling one of their tracksuit legs up and people would be angry with them. Senior players would be judging them, instead of trying to understand what, and why, they were doing it. Their attitude didn't sit well with players and staff, so it was an uphill struggle for them. They were great young players, but without a proper structure around them, without their family to help and guide them, it must have been very difficult.

I think we probably could have done more. They had won the FIFA Under-17s World Cup with France and were named as the best two players in the tournament, and they were cousins. They must have been on top of the world. Gerard actually signed them two years earlier and loaned them back to Le Havre, but when they came to us it must have been a real culture shock. By the time they left us, they hadn't fulfilled their potential in my opinion. From being the next world stars, they left at nowhere near that level and I wouldn't blame Gerard for this as he was one of the best at helping to develop young players.

Steve Finnan was a superb professional. He worked so hard and made the right-back position his own. He was as reliable as they come. Harry Kewell found Liverpool difficult. 'H' had a lot of expectation on him after how well he'd done for Leeds United. If you don't hit the ground running at a club like Liverpool, it's tough, and then he suffered with a lot of injuries. I don't think he hit the heights that he could have reached, but he was a wonderful footballer, no argument there. We often judge individuals in football, but sometimes we can ask the question, 'Could a club have done more to support the player?' I think all clubs, from the top to the bottom of English football, are better equipped now than they were when I was playing. There is more of a support network for players for their on- and off-field lives. There's more duty of care and more strategy associated with player development and that can only be a good thing.

Patrick Berger and Pegguy Arphexad left that summer. Pegguy had really helped me to settle down at the club and he looked out for me. I don't feel that anyone really replaced him in that role for me. I got on with everyone at the club; players, staff and supporters, but I didn't really replace that close bond I had with Pegguy. I wasn't a loner. I would spend time with everyone, but maybe not so much away from the club. I never really had that close friendship at Liverpool. I think that would have helped me if I'd have developed that.

Was I open enough to have close friends? At the start it was tough, but I was soon settled and I feel that this was my shyness coming through and maybe holding me back a little. I should have made more time to make friends with the rest of the squad. In saying that, I've always been comfortable in my own company and with organising my own time. People will often ask, 'Who were your best friends at Liverpool? Who did you get on with?' I got on with everyone, but I didn't live in their lives. As footballers you have a lot of time on your own.

With the national side, for example, I was comfortable on my own in a hotel room, but others really struggled with it. David James wasn't playing in the 2002 World Cup, so he decided to stay awake all night, for 24 hours, to test how he would train the next day without sleep. He did fine, but I think he needed to challenge himself as he was probably bored. I wasn't unhappy at Liverpool, not at all. I loved it there, but could I have done more? Maybe to learn a language, or to take a course? In the American sports system you are going to school as you are playing. I should have made the time to learn more. Thinking too much about football can send you crazy. You need to switch your mind off and do something else.

I think players do this a lot more now, but back then it was frowned upon. Managers probably wouldn't want us doing that kind of thing back then. Channelling your energy elsewhere is a positive. If I had a bad game, I would be down. You can turn to drink. I'm not a big drinker, but I could put some away if I'd played badly. Then the paranoia can kick in. I would drink to numb the disappointment, but I could have focused on education to improve myself and that helps you to prepare for your post-playing career as well.

How can you play football for 20-odd years and then be allowed to leave without a badge, without a qualification? I think it should be mandatory to do something, whether it be coaching, or sport science, or the business side of football. You can give your knowledge back to the game, but also potentially create a career for yourself.

When I look at the number of footballers lost after their playing days; in financial trouble, bankrupt in some cases, without a career or purpose, maybe they've let themselves go a little, it makes me very sad and more should be done to help them. You can say they have money and it's their fault, but if all they've known is playing football since they were a kid, then are we really surprised that it happens time and time again? After training, a lot of the guys would play golf. I don't know about the bookies or going to the pub, as things were more professional by then than my Leicester days. Myself, I would go home, watch some television, wait for the kids to finish school and I would get on with being a dad and living a normal, pretty quiet life.

We didn't win anything in my final season. We reached the UEFA Cup fourth round, beating Olimpija Ljubljana, Steaua Bucharest, Levski Sofia and were knocked out by a Didier Drogba-inspired Marseille. I scored in the away leg, but he scored in both, in a 3-2 aggregate win for them. He was seen as being a talented young player, but he was the same age as me. I had been on the scene with Leicester and England by then, so people probably thought I was getting on a bit. We were knocked out of the domestic cups, finished fourth in the league and qualified for the Champions League. I made 47 appearances and scored 12 goals, which wasn't too bad a return.

Rick Parry, Liverpool's chief executive officer, sat me down at the end of the season and explained that the club were bringing in Djibril Cisse. It felt strange to be told in that manner. I explained that I was fine with that, that I would stay and fight for my place in the team. I didn't want to leave and I'd retained my place when numerous strikers had been signed over previous seasons. Nothing fazed me and I was ready for a battle.

Rick wasn't having any of it. He told me that I wouldn't be playing and that it was over. When someone says that to you, you know there's no way out of it but to leave. You aren't wanted anymore. Game over. When I look back at that, perhaps I was hasty. I had a contract and if I'd have stayed, as fate would have it with other injuries, I would have played anyway. But you can't really think like that though. It's football and you move on.

I signed for Birmingham City for £6.25m within days of the season ending. Gerard left the club a month later and was replaced by Rafa Benitez. I didn't have any idea that was happening. The club had told me that Birmingham were interested, so I went to meet with Steve Bruce, someone who had done it all in the game, and everything was fine. I signed and it all happened so quickly. I bumped into the respected Spanish journalist Guillem Balague after a game in the media mixed zone, and he told me how I'd made a mistake, that Rafa loves to play with a targetman and that I would have loved to play for him. It was too late for me to think like that. I had committed to Birmingham and I wasn't someone who lives in the past and regrets things.

Birmingham were not as big a club as Liverpool, of course, and I was gutted to leave. I was actually speaking to AC Milan at one stage, but nothing came of that. It would have been an incredible opportunity, and I'd started to think about the logistics of it, before it petered out. It did me a favour as that would have been a tough decision to make.

Players didn't want to leave England and move abroad. It would have been a special experience for me but it wasn't to be. Martin was interested in taking me to Celtic, but I didn't fancy that. With no disrespect, I felt that beyond the Old Firm derby, there wasn't much else to make me want to play there. Celtic and Rangers are great clubs, but I didn't want to move to Scotland. Martin tried to persuade me, but I wasn't keen. I loved playing for him, but that wasn't enough for me.

I was excited to be joining Birmingham and to be staying in the Premier League. When a club and a manager want you, you want to repay their faith. I was also excited about moving back to the Midlands, a place I was familiar with. I lived in Birmingham city centre at first and then later in Meriden, not too far from Coventry. Little did I know when I first moved that, despite being nearer to my home in Leicester, I would end up missing the North West and would move back there and settle near to Manchester in the future.

I wasn't surprised to leave Liverpool. I know I was playing regularly, but when you are at a club like that, your standards have to be the absolute highest. If you drop, even a bit, you are at risk of losing your place or leaving. It is very demanding. You have one game, and if you play badly you are out. It drove me and motivated me most of the time, but on occasions it would piss me off. When it comes down to it I am a human being, not a robot. I will make mistakes. I will wake up on the wrong side of the bed. I will be tired. We don't tend to be very understanding of sportspeople underperforming. It happens.

We all have off days. It's more a case of how you bounce back and prove yourself in the next game.

I look back at my time at Liverpool with real pride. It was disappointing to finish my final season without winning anything, but we won six trophies in my four-and-a-bit seasons at the club. I would have snapped your hand off for that at the start. Liverpool fans were always so supportive of me. The media would question my goals-to-games ratio and that would perhaps sway some people's minds, but I always felt that I had the fans' backing. I think that people know that I gave my all for the club and that I cared. I hope they feel like that anyway. I contributed towards a successful period in our history, and worked well with all the strikers I played with, especially Michael Owen, of course.

People would probably say that it was a weird relationship that Michael and I had. On the pitch it was as perfect as it could be. Off the pitch we didn't really have a relationship as such. We were friends, I liked him and I like him to this day, but it comes back to me perhaps not being as available to everyone in order to develop a friendship.

If Michael needed me, he'd know I would be there for him. At Liverpool, we probably had pockets of friends within the group; the Czech lads, the French lads, the English lads, but I didn't really hang around socially with any of them. We were work colleagues.

On the pitch, Michael and I just clicked. The dynamics of the big man, little man worked very well in that era of the game. We both understood, very naturally, where the other one would be. It worked without us having to work at it, if that makes sense. I knew, for example, if I flicked the ball on, he would be there. It was almost instinctive. It probably helped that we had played together for the England under-18s, when he was just 16, and once for the under-21s too. Perhaps Nicolas Anelka would be the best talent I played alongside and Alan Shearer would be the best goalscorer, but Michael was the player I enjoyed playing alongside the most as it worked so well.

We have continued our double act after retiring, as we got together a year or two ago for a Christmas Q&A and the old magic was still there. We also laced up our boots to play in the Star Sixes together and won the tournament, and his little bit of handbags with Jason McAteer made me laugh! Obviously, he has been kind enough to contribute some words to this book too, which I'm humbled by.

The other two big characters from my time at the club and beyond were Jamie Carragher and Steven Gerrard. Carra is a Scouser through and through. When I was at Leicester and started to play for England under-16s, he was the main centre-forward. I was on the bench. He was very talented, alongside a lad called Andy Ducros who was a top player for his age. Fast forward two years and Carra was a centre-back. He was commanding, outspoken and would demand the best from everyone. He was a natural organiser, which you need to have in that position and he turned out to be one of the best ever for Liverpool. He had his issues with some of the lads who would come into the club and perhaps not match his work-rate. He would want everyone to get stuck in and work hard, but some of the foreign lads would pull out of a tackle if they didn't fancy it and Carra would let them know that wasn't acceptable. Dioufy and him didn't see eye-to-eye for example, but that's not really a surprise to anyone as not many people saw eye-to-eye with Dioufy. I don't think he was big enough or good enough to dictate his own behaviour and didn't conform to the standards set by people like Carra and Stevie.

Stevie was nurtured by Gerard Houllier and, I believe, Gary McAllister. I don't think it's any surprise that Stevie took Macca to Glasgow Rangers as his assistant. Macca was someone that everyone looked up to. I'd had Walshy, Lenny, those kind of senior players looking after me at Leicester, and now at Liverpool, we all had Macca. We could see that Stevie was being groomed to be the leader, the talisman of the club and he became that and more. He represented everything that Liverpool Football Club stood for and I'm sure he will go on to be a success as a manager too.

If I'd have stayed another year at Liverpool, that would have been perfect. The club went on to win the Champions League and I would have loved to have been involved in that. Who knows though, maybe if I'd stayed we wouldn't have won it. One small thing can change the course of history. It's not a regret though. I look back and I feel two things: love and joy. Overwhelming love and joy that I was able to play for such a magnificent football club. Yes, I had some lows at the start, such as my feelings of alienation, but I got over them relatively quickly. They were brought on by other factors, but the football was always great.

I joined Liverpool to better myself and to win things. Yes, the money was there, but there was no point to it all if we didn't win trophies and create memories. That's what I look back and remember anyway. If I had to have one regret, it would be the way it ended for Gerard Houllier, as he was sacked from a role he loved. Even the way he departed was with dignity. He's a wonderful man and a wonderful manager. He took Liverpool on to another level and I believe, especially from the supporters, he gets the credit that he deserves for everything he did. He is a special man.

I love going back to Liverpool and working for LFCTV and doing bits of media work for the club. It's nice to retain that relationship and to go back and watch games. It's very nice to be asked by them. They look after their ex-players very well and that's in keeping with the way the club is run.

I don't think I realised how well loved I was at Liverpool until I returned as a player with other clubs, as well as coming back as a guest after my playing days. It really hit me. I knew I was supported and they appreciated what I was trying to do, despite the media trying to persuade people to think differently. They are influential as well, so you do worry a little that people may buy into the media agendas. I came back with Bolton Wanderers as a player and the whole stadium stood up, applauded and sang my name. I was choked up. It took my breath away. Even now, I'll bump into Liverpool fans and they'll remember a goal, a game, a moment from my career and will tell me all about it and where they were in the stadium at the time. It's nice. It means a lot to me that I was out on the pitch doing something I loved, making others happy. I'm a small part of the history of a quite outstanding football club and a community of people, and that makes me proud.

It's a football club that simply never leaves your heart.

CHAPTER EIGHT

62

MY international career should have started as a 15-year-old, attending trials at Lilleshall. If successful, players resided there and formed part of the England Schoolboys squad, feeding into the England youth set-up. My mum had other ideas though. She wasn't happy with the thought of me being away from home at that age and wanted me to carry on at school, so that was a nonstarter for me. Life has a funny way of working out though. I was at Leicester City's school of excellence anyway, but if I'd have gone through the England Schoolboys system, I would have most likely been poached by a bigger club. Most of the lads in that system were playing for teams like Manchester United, Liverpool and Arsenal, and I don't think Leicester would have been able to hold on to me. I'm pleased with how it worked out as I wanted to play for Leicester above all else at that time.

My England age group was full of talented players who went on to make it as professionals: Jamie Carragher, Marlon Broomes, Andy Ducros, Wes Brown was a little younger, Gavin McCann and Nigel Quashie. Nigel was technically, at that age, as good a passer as I'd played with. It wasn't clear which foot he was best with; he was excellent.

I was invited to an England under-16 trial game. I had to grow up fast. I'd have to make my own way to Lilleshall on the train, which was Leicester to Birmingham New Street and then change for a train to Stafford, before getting a taxi to Lilleshall. I was still a kid, so it was an adventure for me, helping to take me out of the comfort zone of my hometown.

Trials are strange environments. Everyone is out to impress. It's not a regular environment. I felt that my game suited the philosophy of those watching, as I was a team player, not just trying to show my individual skills. After doing enough to be selected, I went with England under-16s to the Euros in the Republic of Ireland. It was a tough challenge. The technical standards of those I was playing alongside and against was a step up from what I was used to at club youth level, even though I was playing at under-18s level for Leicester.

It wasn't daunting, but it was an eye-opener and while I felt I was okay, there were others who were exceptional. I only got four caps for England at that level, all of which came in that tournament. My debut was against Portugal in a 1-0 win and then I made my first start against the hosts, Ireland, before facing Czechoslovakia, and then we were knocked out in the quarter-finals against Ukraine on penalties. My overriding memory is of being tired. After the game against Ireland, one of the coaches asked me hypothetically if I could have played the next day if we had a game, and honestly and perhaps naively, I said I couldn't. I was in bits from playing these games, with maybe one day of rest and then back to training. It was pretty demanding for me at that age, but I loved the honour of playing for England.

Around 18 months later, I was called up to the England under-18s squad, so I must have been doing something right. I made my debut against Latvia in the qualifiers for the 1996 under-18 Euros, scoring both goals in a 2-0 win. We qualified for the tournament and won the third-place play-off against a Belgium side which included Emile Mpenza.

It was the tournament where I first played alongside Michael Owen; the start of a special partnership in my career which was continued at senior England level. Michael was just 16 years old. We also had Rio Ferdinand, John Curtis, Stephen Clemence and Richard Wright, but the tournament was won by a very good French side, which included Thierry Henry. It was also the tournament that Gerard Houllier first saw Michael and I play together, which must have stuck with him four years later when he reunited us by signing me from Leicester.

When the Euros were over, we were all partying in a nightclub in France. Typically, everyone was drinking, even though we were all under age. I looked over at one point and the French squad were all there too, but they were just drinking water. Soon after, we were outside in the car park, kicking a ball around, running over car roofs, being stupid. There was a craze at the time to rip people's shirts open, so we were stumbling around with our shirts hanging off us. The French lads were looking over wondering what the hell was going on.

* * *

After that summer, in October 1996, I was playing for the under-21s at the age of 18, making my debut against Poland, and in May 1997 I scored my first goal at that level, against Poland as well. My final game for the under-21s was against the Federal Republic of Yugoslavia in March 2000. The game was played at Barcelona B's stadium, next to Camp Nou, and had been delayed for months due to political tension in Belgrade.

We won 3-0 to qualify for the Euros that summer, but my memory of the game was of being racially abused by one supporter in the crowd. It was different to having hundreds or even thousands of people shout abuse at you. This was personal. One man. I could see him and I could hear him clearly. He called me Kunta Kinte, the character from *Roots*, nigger and made gorilla noises and gestures at me. At one point the game was stopped and the referee went over to get him to stop the abuse.

If it happened now he would have been removed and banned, but even then, in 2000, things were brushed under the carpet a little. I was spat at by someone at the age of 16, as I warmed up for England, and called a nigger, but this was different; it was constant, not a one-off incident. There was at least 30 minutes of this guy hurling abuse at me. I was distracted, I couldn't help it. One lone voice, in a quiet stadium had more effect on me than a whole stand would have done. I didn't feel I had to prove anything to him though. It didn't motivate me to do better, to score to shut him up or anything like that. He was ignorant, an absolute disgrace, and while we won comfortably that day, I will always remember how I was treated. People would say that these countries didn't have many black people in them, but I couldn't accept that as a reasonable excuse. This was ignorance and hatred and it was one of the worst experiences of my career.

* * *

Overall, I loved my time with the under-21s. Playing at youth level for England really helped me to prepare for playing at senior level. I found the style of international football, the patient nature of it, very different to playing at club level, and the challenge of tournaments was another element I had to get used to. I played 17 times for the under-21s, and nearly 30 times in total at youth level, with many of those games alongside the likes of Carra, Frank Lampard, Rio Ferdinand and Michael Carrick. I only played once with Michael for the under-21s, as he had already made it to the senior squad. We had lost 2-0 to Greece away in a European Championship 1998 play-off first leg. We beat them 4-2 at Carrow Road in the return leg; I scored twice and Michael once, but we were knocked out on away goals. We grew together as a group at youth level though, and we progressed individually through the system. Ultimately, we didn't win anything at senior level, which was a disappointment to everyone, but I still believe in young players representing England at age-group level to help them prepare for the big stage.

The coaching that we received at international youth level was very high too. I particularly enjoyed working under Peter Taylor. He was an excellent coach. He didn't do well at Leicester City after Martin left, but managing and coaching are two completely different things. He worked us hard on our movement and interchanging of positions with the midfielders and wingers. I hadn't done that kind of thing before, so I enjoyed the fresh approach.

Things moved quickly for me with England though. I was just 19 when Glenn Hoddle called me into the England senior squad for a game against Moldova. I didn't play, but it was another step forward and more experience for me. I played against Chile for England B in a friendly a year later, and scored, but it was another year until Howard Wilkinson called me up for a friendly against France, after Glenn had left the role.

I thought that Glenn was a superb coach. I don't know how others felt about him, but it was weird for me personally, as he never really spoke to me. The only time he did speak to me of any note was in a training session when he told me in no uncertain terms that I needed to get on the ball. The tempo of his sessions was always really high. Some players can be insecure when a manager doesn't speak to them, but it never really bothered me. I knew I must have been doing something right as I had been called up for my country. I was young, and I was happy to learn and be a part of it. I never took anything too personally.

Glenn Roeder would lead the training for Hoddle, with John Gorman in the background. I liked the way training was set up. I wasn't the kind of character to go around demanding the ball and swearing at people who were much more experienced than me though. That squad was packed full of big names: Ian Wright, Alan Shearer, Paul Gascoigne, Paul Ince, Tony Adams, David Seaman, Gareth Southgate and Stan Collymore, to name a few. They all welcomed me. I feel the senior pros at that time were better than perhaps in the era after. They would sit down and talk to you and give you time as a younger lad. I really appreciated that. Martin Keown was brilliant, as was Southgate. They would listen and support you, and it's no surprise to see that both of them have gone on to be successful after their playing days finished.

When people look back at Hoddle's time in charge, they will often mention the faith healer, Eileen Drewery. I met Eileen. If you are going to make something like that work for you, you have to believe in it. I remember Robbie Fowler coming out laughing after seeing Eileen, saying that she had identified that he had demons. For me, I look at those type of things and probably have more belief in them now than I did back then. From the age of nine, I was used to a system that dealt with injuries in a medical and professional way. Eileen, however, held my ankle and made calming noises, so this was unconventional, shall we say. My ankle didn't feel any better or any worse, but I think Glenn was looking at getting players to offload their problems to Eileen, perhaps ahead of his time as we have sports psychologists who perform that function now. If Glenn had called it that, perhaps there wouldn't have been such an issue, I don't know. I didn't feel that anyone really bought into it with Glenn. He was definitely ahead of his time, but maybe it wasn't communicated and handled correctly with the players, the media and the fans. There was just an awkwardness to it all.

I wasn't star-struck by playing and training alongside the big names of English football. That came earlier when I was with the under-21s and we would travel with the seniors to an away game and play the night before. Then, I'd be stood open-mouthed, looking at Wrighty and Gazza as we flew on the same plane as them. Ian Wright was the one for me; he was brilliant and I really looked up to him. We would even travel to games with members of the media as well, which helped to get a relationship started with them, building a trust, and it prepared you for their role within the game.

Glenn left after his alleged comments regarding disabled people, which became a huge media scandal, meaning he lost his job for his views, rather than his football management ability. You have to be so careful what you say, and the comments you make will evoke reactions from people. If he did make those comments, he shouldn't have. It's as simple as that. You are accountable, particularly in a role like that and there was no option but for him to leave.

Howard Wilkinson stepped in and it was tough for him, in that temporary role. His training sessions were quite innovative whenever I played under him; he would have these huge speakers dotted around the side of the pitch, and he would be linked up to them, so he could get his messages across to us loud and clear. He'd walk around with his headset on, shouting about our shape, and stopping training to pick out certain patterns of play. Those headsets pick up everything though, and every now and again, he would hack up a mouthful of phlegm, spitting it on to the turf and the noise of it would scream out around the pitch. We would all be looking around at each other, laughing. His training was good though, and he was always looking at other clubs and countries and trying to adopt some of their ideas, which was impressive.

I finally made my debut for England in April 1999, in a friendly against Hungary in Budapest, under the new manager Kevin Keegan. I replaced Kevin Phillips late on, who was one of five debutants that night, the others being Wes Brown, Jamie Carragher and Michael Gray.

It was a huge honour to come on, even for a few minutes. I'd been around the England set-up for a long time, so I was desperate to get my first senior cap. My family took it all in their stride. They seemed to know what I was going to do from the start and there was no real celebration or surprise element to it all. They just expected me to go on and do more. I never doubted myself either. I always say that to young players now; don't beat yourself up and don't doubt yourself. With belief, you are halfway there.

Later in 1999, I came on as a substitute at the Stadium of Light against Belgium in a 2-1 win, a game that my then Leicester team-mate, Steve Guppy, made his one England appearance in. Muzzy Izzet was linked with the England side at that time, but ended up playing for Turkey as Keegan didn't select him. Gupps was nervous as I've said before. Playing in the England B side with him, he would beat himself up before and after. I felt for him as it's horrible to see people in that frame of mind, suffering from anxiety, but he was a good guy and he had a career he can be proud of.

I was part of the squad which went to Scotland for the first leg of the play-offs for Euro 2000. I was sitting on the bench at Hampden Park and that was amazing. I think you have to actually travel to Scotland for an England game to realise how fierce the rivalry is. You can't comprehend it until you experience it. They were coming for us, on and off the field. We won 2-0 there, with both goals from Paul Scholes, and I managed to come on as a sub in the second leg, which we lost 1-0, but went through anyway. Stuart Campbell, my Leicester team-mate was goading me, saying they were going to batter us, but he did love the fact that I was part of the England side as he was a good friend.

My first England start came in February 2000 against Argentina at Wembley, ahead of the Euros that summer. That was a big moment for me, no doubt about it. I jumped up and landed awkwardly on my back during the game, and I can remember Martin O'Neill saying how scared he was that I wouldn't get back up, as the following Sunday Leicester were playing Tranmere in the League Cup Final. People told me that the pubs of Leicester were packed with fans watching me, which was really special to hear and meant a great deal.

Years later, I met a journalist who was working in London and was close to the Argentina coaching staff at the time of the game. He was sent to do some spying on us and to report back. He told them that I wouldn't play that night, that I was big and not that fast, and that we already had Shearer and we would partner him with Phillips. They apparently built their preparations around me not playing, so I had an element of surprise about me that night.

Despite the game finishing 0-0, I ripped their defence apart, so much so that their experienced captain Roberto Sensini was subbed off after half an hour. I doubt the journalist was asked for his scouting help ever again. I was replaced by Andy Cole late on, which was also an honour in itself. I had cramp as I'd run too much, and the crowd actually booed the decision as they wanted me to stay on. It was one of those nights, where I had the pace of the defence and I was too strong for them.

If I'm honest, even though I liked all of the England managers I played for, Kevin was the one I had the weakest relationship with. I felt that with younger players, he would really attack us verbally. He would be really harsh yet would treat the senior players much better, with respect and no blame. He never said a cross word to them. I wasn't the only young player who felt like that either. I don't know why he was like that, as he'd been a young player with expectation on him as well during his playing days, so he should have understood how we all felt.

In the Euros, when Michael scored against Romania, if you watch it back you can see the reaction of the squad, jumping on him and celebrating. That was in direct response to the way that Keegan had treated him, I believe. I couldn't understand why you would be like that with Michael, knocking his confidence. If you were trying to get the best out of someone, battering them is not the way. I know managers have to be tough, but he took it too far in my opinion. It was all a bit weird if I'm honest.

I scored my first goal against Malta ahead of the Euros and I always felt confident that I would be picked for the tournament, as I was versatile and different to the other strikers in the squad. I could play out wide, up front or in behind, and could have an impact coming off the bench. When I look back at that era, Andy Cole was the striker who I was surprised never did better for England, as his goal record in the league and in European football was simply incredible.

I loved Euro 2000. I know it was a poor tournament for us, but the training and being around the lads in that environment for the first time was something I will never forget. I was still young, so while I was gutted that we didn't get past the group stages, I felt like I would have time to be successful. I got myself in a bit of trouble for speaking out and being a bit naive though. We had a games room, full of free stuff from sponsors, and I was asked about the room by the media and I said, 'I don't know anything about it. I don't think anyone goes in there to be honest.'

The sponsors went crazy and the media picked up on it. Keegan had a right go at me. I'd just told the truth. I should have just said that everyone loved it, but I wasn't experienced in handling the media and in thinking ahead about the consequences of what you say to them. All the stuff in the games room was given to us for free, so they wanted us to say how great it all was. I guess I wasn't a good liar.

I felt like we were very tired in Euro 2000. That was the only conclusion I could come to. It's not an excuse, it's my opinion. Mentally and physically we were drained from the Premier League, with no break and the other sides looked fresher. We tired during the Portugal game, when we were 2-0 up and lost 3-2. We beat Germany, who had a bad tournament, and then lost 3-2 late on against Romania, who knocked us out. Keegan could have been more supportive, but then the players in that era didn't mope or moan, we just got on with it. The senior pros were strong characters and they would take the lead on things anyway.

The negativity of the tournament carried on into the crucial 2002 World Cup qualifier against Germany in October 2000. It was a significant game; the last at the old Wembley Stadium. I was on the bench, an unused sub. As everyone remembers, Keegan quit in the post-match interviews following a 1-0 defeat. It must have been very sad for him, as he realised he had taken the side as far as he could. He wore his heart on his sleeve, and wouldn't have hung on just for the sake of it. He put England's interests first, which should be admired.

He was emotional that day. Kevin was a great player and did well as a manager too, particularly with Newcastle. I found out he had quit from one of the other lads, while still sitting in the dressing room. It was a strangely eerie atmosphere. Everyone was very sad that afternoon. No one wanted to lose that game and I think that the weight of the occasion weighed on Kevin as well as it did the players. I am grateful to him for giving me my debut and he allowed me freedom to express myself under him too.

Wilkinson was in charge for our 0-0 draw in Finland and then Taylor took the reins for the 1-0 defeat away to Italy in a friendly, where David Beckham was famously given the captain's armband for the first time. There was a minute's silence at the game, as a mark of respect for a tragedy in the

Agnelli family, who were associated with Juventus and the game was hosted at their ground. We were all told the protocol before the game, but when the referee blew the whistle, I went in to autopilot and ran towards the centre circle to line up, as we do here. However, we had been told to just stand in our positions on the pitch. I looked like an idiot running around while everyone else was motionless. I stopped and just put my head down and wanted the ground to swallow me up.

People often say that Becks was an obvious choice for captain, but Sol Campbell was a strong candidate too, and it's something he mentioned himself in the media. He was a captain at Arsenal and was a strong centre-back, part of the Invincibles side, so he had a point. However, it was clear which route England were going in and Beckham, as we now know, had an incredible commercial appeal as well as his on-field skills and leadership qualities. In the 2002 World Cup, Becks had four security men allocated just to him and hundreds of fans would follow us around Japan, locals by the way, just to get a glimpse of him. It was Beckham-mania and we had never seen anything like it ourselves as players. Grown men would copy his haircut, running after our bus with a Mohican on their head. It was unreal. Sol was a good leader himself though, but Taylor made his decision and it stuck.

Sven-Göran Eriksson was appointed as England manager in July 2001, leaving his role at Lazio in Italy and I played and scored in his first game, a 3-0 friendly win over Spain at Villa Park. Sven was very different to Keegan. He was similar in his approach to Houllier for me. Everything was structured. He'd put his whiteboard up and move his magnets, representing players, around for 20 minutes showing what he wanted from you. I liked that. I wanted structure and his way suited me, but it perhaps wouldn't work for everyone.

At Liverpool, we would go through every opposition player meticulously, even if we were playing a lower league side, and Sven was like that. He had Steve McClaren on his coaching staff and he was excellent; a very good coach. Sven was at every game possible, watching players and it was often shown on television. Chris Powell was picked for the Spain game, and it showed to people that no matter how old you were, if you were playing well, you would get a chance regardless of reputation. I enjoyed playing for Sven. One of his biggest challenges was to keep everyone happy. He had so many good players to pick from and if you weren't playing, I'm not sure he kept you happy and motivated as he would just focus on those involved in the starting 11. I understand that, but he had quality players on the bench or left out and that was difficult for him.

Everything was relaxed under Sven. Becks would act as the communicator and would tell us all where we were going and what we were doing. We often did activities together as a group after training; eating out, shopping, team bonding. I liked that. I always remember Becks having a deal with Armani and he'd turn up with a huge box of stuff they'd given him, but he'd give it out to the squad and share everything.

That was the way he operated, always trying to put others first.

I've written about the 5-1 win in Germany already. It was revenge for the defeat at the old Wembley, and it was a truly magical night. Despite reaching three quarter-finals it was probably a high point for Sven in his time as England manager. It was certainly the best win I was involved in. We had to go behind and do it the hard way. That was England all over.

It was easy to think that we had already qualified for the World Cup in South Korea and Japan after that game. We just had to beat Albania and then draw with Greece, both at home. We cruised the first one, but came unstuck at Old Trafford against the Greeks, who twice went ahead. This was the game that really stamped Becks's profile on world football. His free kick in injury time was as perfect a set piece as you could wish to take. It's not a nice situation when all you need is a draw in a game. It makes players question themselves and they play within their capabilities. It's a strange feeling. That day, even discounting the remarkable goal, Becks carried the nation on his shoulders. He was everywhere on the pitch, making tackles at full-back, driving through midfield, swinging crosses over from the wing. It was like watching a real-life Roy of the Rovers. I've never seen a player control a game from the wing like that. He was brilliant. It was an iconic goal and his celebration will always be remembered too. He gave energy to us and made us believe that we were never beaten and could go to the World Cup and achieve something special.

We warmed up with a few games; the 1-1 in Holland is best rembered for Darius Vassell scoring with an overhead kick. Darius was extremely quiet, but he was strong and was a very good player. I'm not saying he didn't have good players around him at Aston Villa, but playing for England seemed to bring the best out of him. He moved the ball well, had quick feet and Sven loved him. We then lost to Italy before travelling to the World Cup where we drew with South Korea and Cameroon. Those games were to help us acclimatise to the conditions as it was very hot and humid. South Korea, in particular, were much quicker than us. We just weren't used to playing in that kind of weather. It was a real eye-opener.

Japan was amazing. What a country. The tournament was organised perfectly. We would travel on the bullet train, yet the phone technology was that far ahead of ours that our mobiles didn't work out there. I had been to Asia before with Liverpool, but not to Japan and it was something else. The stadiums were immaculate, purpose-built for the tournament. There was a lot of downtime away from training and games, but as we were in an alien country, so to speak, on the other side of the world, it was difficult to just go out and live a normal life.

We were often stuck in the hotel, which didn't really bother me as I was fine in my own company, but I know that some of the lads found it frustrating. Sven again encouraged

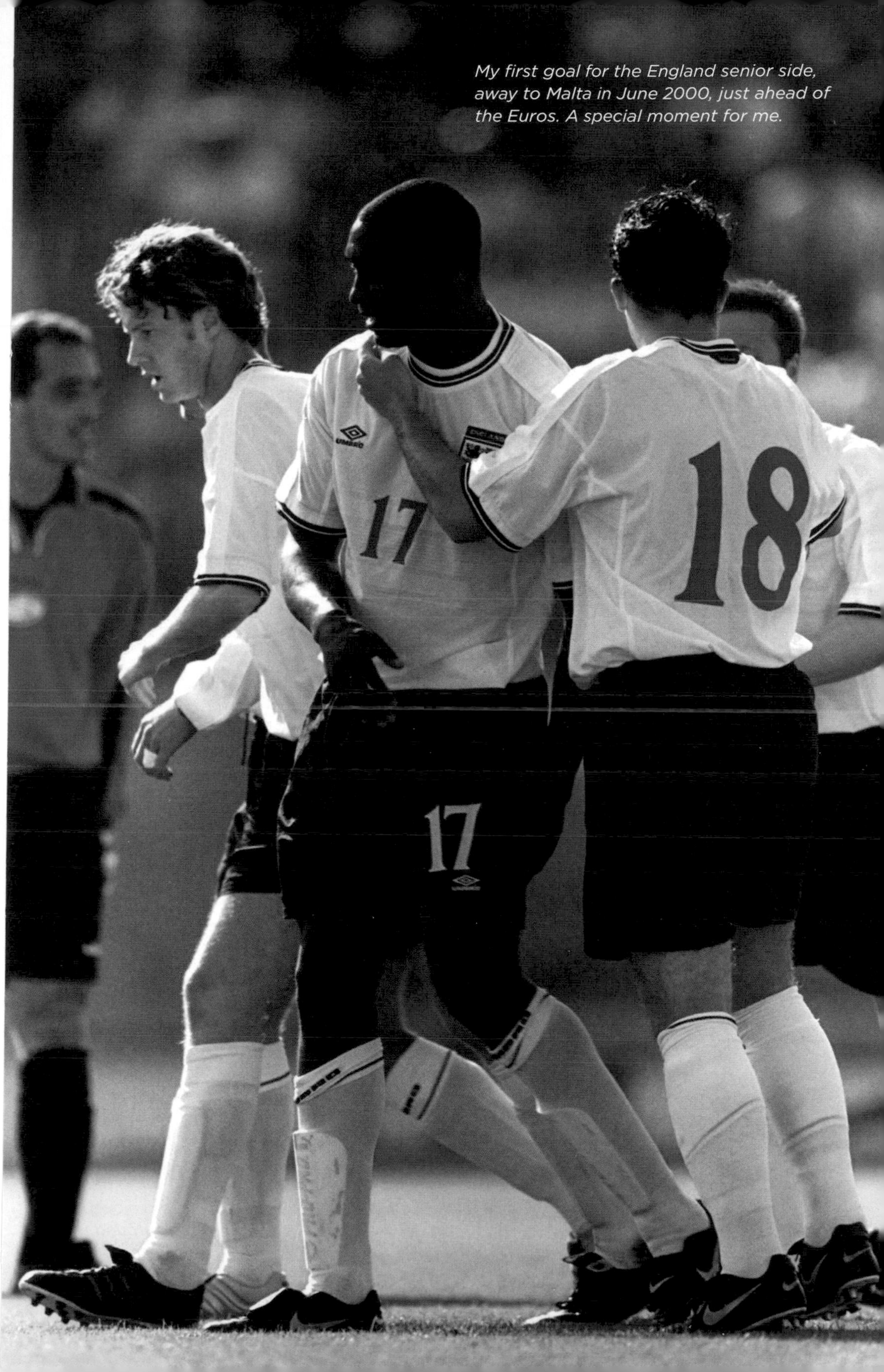

My first goal for the England senior side, away to Malta in June 2000, just ahead of the Euros. A special moment for me.

England vs Sweden, opening game of Group F, 2002 World Cup, back row left to right: Heskey, Campbell, Seaman, R. Ferdinand, Mills, Owen. Front row left to right: Vassell, Hargreaves, Scholes, Beckham, A. Cole.

A goal in a World Cup. The stuff dreams are made of. I scored against Denmark in the last 16 of the 2002 World Cup, in a 3-0 win. I would have loved to have seen that celebration a few more times for my country.

The dream is over. I wasn't ready to come home and I felt this was our best chance of winning a trophy. We gave everything but we ran out of steam. That was a quality Brazil side and even with ten men, they were a real force.

Wayne Rooney exploded on to the international football stage and became a true England great. From the Turkey game, where he charged at them like a bull, to Euro 2004 and becoming the top scorer, he had a career to remember. Wayne was great to play alongside and a real character too.

El Hadji Diouf was undoubtedly a talented player, capable of extraordinary skill and sublime game-changing moments. Sadly, he was never far away from controversy. Dioufy craved the attention and the limelight; an extroverted guy, who would perform to an audience, but was totally different in private.

Our opening game of Euro 2004 was very nearly a famous victory, but turned in to an agonising defeat. Zinedine Zidane's two late goals won the game, and France went on to win the group. This was my last game in an England shirt under Sven.

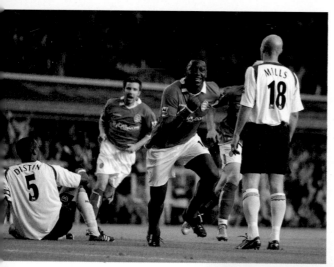

Off and running. My first goal for my new club, Birmingham City, came against Manchester City. My old Leicester team-mate, Muzzy Izzet is pictured in the background. Muzzy was sensational for Leicester, a real fan favourite with skills, goals, energy, he had everything. Birmingham fans were unlucky not to see the best of him as a result of injuries.

Birmingham derby day. Scoring against Aston Villa really endeared me to the Blues fans. The atmosphere was lively that day and whilst my goal wasn't the prettiest, squirming under Thomas Sorensen's body, it still meant a lot to me, and to the fans as the photo shows.

us to do stuff together and he was relaxed and happy to go with the flow, but there was only so much we could do. I'd have my *Def Comedy Jam* DVDs on and that would keep me happy.

We had our own chef with us, so didn't really sample the local cuisine. Everything was planned out for us. If we went to an event, we would let Becks walk ahead of us, with the security, and then we'd follow behind without any fuss. Anything that guy touched just turned to gold. There was great respect for him as well. Those that knew him well, the United lads, would probably have a bit of banter with him, but everyone liked and respected him. He was a very good captain and a great guy to be around. Even now, when I see him, he'll be really nice. That seems to surprise people. My wife commented on what a nice, polite guy he was, having time to talk to us. It's just the way he is. He's still the same person, despite becoming one of the most famous people on the planet.

Our tournament began with a draw against Sweden, before Becks's penalty saw us past Argentina, which laid the ghosts of his sending-off in the 1998 World Cup to rest. We drew 0-0 with Nigeria and qualified for the last 16. I managed to score against Denmark in a 3-0 win to set us up to play Brazil in the quarter-finals. That was a real dream, to score in a World Cup and to be facing one of the world's great football nations.

I feel like people look back at that tournament for an answer as to why we lost to Brazil. This is how I see it: we went 1-0 up and could have gone on to win, but they had three players who went on to win the Ballon d'Or in that squad – Rivaldo, Ronaldo and Ronaldinho – and Roberto Carlos came second. That's not an excuse, but I think we perhaps forget what an excellent side that was, and they went on to win the trophy. I still think it was a chance missed, but I know in the dressing room that we left everything out there and at the end we were gutted and exhausted. I wasn't ready to come home. Some of the older guys were even more distraught, knowing that it was their last chance to win something with England.

There was a feeling in the group that we could build on that World Cup and have a real go at winning Euro 2004. We had no reason to fear anyone. We beat Turkey 2-0 at the Stadium of Light in qualifying and Wayne Rooney really announced himself that night with a display beyond his years. I was left out for Wayne to play alongside Michael Owen. He was amazing. So strong, like a bull just knocking them all over the place.

After that game, in April 2003, we had a summer tour to South Africa and I managed to score against them, but the trip was more memorable for us all having the chance to meet the great man, Nelson Mandela. It was a real honour for me, the first time I had ever been to Africa. Mr Mandela may have been older by then, but he had an amazing aura about him, even then. Having him and Becks together in one room made sure that we were all the sidekicks! It was like being a support act for The Beatles or something! I was cool with that. I was very excited about meeting him and, unsurprisingly, we were all trying to nudge people out of the way to get nearer to him, which comes across in the photos as well. He did so much for people, not just in his country but across the world. He must have been so scared, but he kept his belief throughout his ordeal in prison and fought for what he knew was fair and right. He will be talked about throughout history, forever, so I felt privileged to be in a room with him. It was a humbling moment for us all. Thankfully, my kids will never have to experience that level of abuse, and in a large way that is down to him.

That June I received another honour, by playing for England at Leicester's then Walkers Stadium, and I got to wear the captain's armband for part of the game after Michael went off. We won 2-1 and that was a very proud night for me and my family. I'm pretty sure I could have sold the stadium out myself with requests from friends and family. I had people asking for 10, 20, 30 tickets, but I couldn't accommodate them all. It was a great experience to be back in my city, and for people to see me wearing the Three Lions. My family were there and they loved it. I had the armband on for 15 minutes and played alongside Rooney. I would have loved to have scored. A photo from that night is etched into a glass door in my home, alongside some other images from my career, but that is an evening I will never forget.

Those games were part of our preparation for the final group game, away to Turkey. We needed a draw to qualify for Euro 2004 and knew they would make it very difficult for us. It was a loud and hostile atmosphere. Becks slipped and missed a penalty in the first half and Alpay poked him after it. He continued that by jabbing Becks in the face as we all ran towards the tunnel at half-time and then it turned into complete carnage. I got through the tunnel and was into the breakout area. I looked to my left and saw Hasan Şaş with Ashley Cole. I'd already pushed my way through people and then I saw Şaş spit right in Ashley's face. I ran straight over and slapped him one, right on his face. I saw red. To spit in someone's face is just disgusting. After that, all hell broke loose.

A security guard, in a brown trenchcoat, came steaming over towards us all and grabbed hold of me. I could see him. I braced myself and at the last second I grabbed his coat and pulled it over his head so he couldn't see. Then I started hitting him. I was defending myself. People were coming in at all angles and I was waiting for a hit, but according to others the fight went on all around me, almost like a scene from a cartoon. I was told that Turkish TV caught some of the brawl. There was another fight going on back in the tunnel, involving Wayne and Alpay. I don't know why, but some foreign players seem to resort to spitting as a way to settle disagreements, and I'm sorry, but I'm just not having that.

I was backed by my Liverpool manager Gerard Houllier, who claimed that because of my nature, I must have been provoked. We escaped a charge individually, but both the FA and the Turkish FA were charged. I had to react on the night. I couldn't watch a team-mate be treated like that. I knew what we would face that night as I'd played in Turkey before, but that was just unacceptable. They placed huge speakers in the corners of the ground, near to the pitch, and they created a real noise, even getting those sitting above the away dressing room and dugout to make as much of a sound as possible. There were flares, and the players were trying to provoke us too. We were a team full of big characters though. Sven calmed everyone down at half-time. He didn't lose his temper with us. He spoke softly and reminded us to focus. We held firm and drew 0-0 against a good side to qualify for Portugal 2004.

After the Turkey result, we were hit with a blow which came out of the blue. Rio missed a drugs test at Manchester United and was banned for eight months, meaning he would miss the rest of the Premier League season and the Euros. Gary Neville, who was the self-appointed union representative for us, I guess, urged us all to refuse to play for England to support Rio. I got on well with Gary. I wasn't close with him, but he was a good speaker and he wanted the best for us all. He could be a bit of a busy bastard, as people tend to say in football, but I didn't mind that. I was still a young player in the squad and I just nodded my head and was happy to go along with whatever the rest of the group wanted.

Gary kept pushing us all not to play and I think people didn't feel completely comfortable about it. Everyone liked Rio, but everyone wanted to play. It was a little bit like the

Gary Neville Show, and I guess if Rio had asked us to back him, we would have, without all the threats. Gary has become a great pundit and a good businessman too and I can see why, as he is a very talented communicator.

The group didn't really enjoy a good relationship with the media either, and we'd have all probably pulled out of playing just to piss them off and to stick two fingers up at them. Players can communicate via social media now. Back then, we'd walk in to breakfast and see negative headlines about us every day. It dragged us down and anyone who says otherwise is lying.

Look at Raheem Sterling and the way he was treated by the media, but he has changed the narrative through the good work he does, and by showing people through his own media. We couldn't do any of that. We didn't really know or understand the full story with Rio as well. As I look back now, he missed a drug test and the rules around that are strict. You have to be where you say you are. Once you leave the premises and don't give the test, you have essentially failed it. I believe Rio offered to come back, but by then it was too late.

I have to be honest and say that I was hardly ever tested, perhaps once every 18 months, but then after this happened I seemed to be tested much more often. One year, I went on holiday and I had to provide an hour time slot every day, where I would be available to be tested. I was in Barbados, so for that one hour I had to be in a set place, ready in case they flew out to test me. I had to account for time differences as well as we were a few hours behind. It was very strange. They didn't show up, but they could have, and that's the scrutiny with which you are under.

The Euros themselves were a memorable tournament, with Greece surprising everyone to win it, much in the way that Leicester City won the Premier League in 2016. Our opening game was against France and we were 1-0 ahead before Becks missed a penalty to put us two ahead. Wayne also burst through and could have squared to Darius, so we only had ourselves to blame when the French came back. I gave away a free kick after I came on as a sub for Wayne, which Zinedine Zidane scored, and then we gave away a penalty in injury time after Steven Gerrard's short backpass, and Zidane, who actually puked up as he was setting the ball down, scored the winner. Sven had asked me to sit on the defensive midfielder and help us to hold the lead, but they had Patrick Vieira and Claude Makelele in there. I was a bit clumsy with my challenge. We lost and I never played for Sven again. He picked me in squads again, but the France game was my last under him.

We didn't take our opportunities in the France game and could have been out of sight, but against a side of that quality, who had won tournaments and had world-class players throughout the side, if you don't take your chances they will put you to the sword. Sven never spoke to me about that game. I'm guessing he wasn't happy with me but he never made that clear. The side went on to beat Switzerland 3-0 and Croatia

4-2, before playing the hosts, Portugal, and drawing 2-2 after extra time. Michael put us 1-0 up, Portugal equalised late on and then took the lead in extra-time before Lamps levelled five minutes before the end.

Darius was brought on for Wayne who went off with a foot injury after just 27 minutes. I was left on the bench. I guess that Sven had already made his mind up that he didn't want me involved, as I hadn't played in the previous two games. I couldn't answer the reasons why. I would have loved to have played alongside Michael again that night.

Darius missed his penalty in the shoot-out and we were out, 6-5. He never kicked a ball again for England which must have been awful for him. I didn't complain about not playing. Sven had made his decision and that was it. We had a great side, so I never complained. I just felt so sorry for Darius. In my mind, from what I saw, I didn't feel like he wanted to take the penalty, but he did step up and he should be praised for that. It takes a strong person to do that, in that situation. Becks missed the first penalty in the shoot-out, but no one remembers that really. You always remember the last penalty.

I knew I would play for England again. It wasn't arrogance, it was just self confidence. I was disappointed that it took a while and that I didn't play for Sven again, but that's football. He picked me in three more squads, but I was unused. I did really well in my first season at Birmingham City and it would have been great to represent the club in the England squad, but it wasn't to be.

There were very good players in attacking positions though; obviously Wayne and Michael, but also Peter Crouch and Jermain Defoe. There was also Andrew Johnson and Alan Smith, and of course Theo Walcott who was taken to the World Cup, but I felt like he was more of a winger. For the 2006 World Cup, Sven took Rooney, Owen, Crouch and Walcott, although the young Arsenal signing never played a minute of the tournament.

Once they decided upon Crouchy, I was never going to get a look-in, as you'd only take one big man. I felt for Jermain to be honest. I think he should have gone to that tournament as he was firing at that time, and he would have fitted in well. Wayne was injured for the early part, recovering from a broken foot, and Michael went off injured in the Sweden game and didn't play again in the tournament. It was frustrating to watch, but I kept my belief that I would play my part again in future England teams.

I liked playing for Sven. I think his off-field antics overshadowed his time as England manager unfortunately. That became news and the focus of the media, especially back then. The media loved it. I can't recall us as players talking about it. Perhaps some of the guys did, but it didn't interest me at all. It wasn't my business. It's sad really. In Italy or France, a coach's private life wasn't deemed newsworthy, but over here, it became front page news and made Sven one of the main talking points in the country at the time. The spotlight on him was unbelievable. The papers would talk about who he was with, what she was wearing, and very little about the actual football. I couldn't get my head around it. We were doing well on the pitch on the whole and the public seemed to really like him.

We should have won something under Sven though, no doubt about it. The 2002 World Cup was the one for me. I wasn't ready to go home and felt that was our time, but we could have won Euro 2004 or the 2006 World Cup, which I know was the one Sven felt was the missed opportunity. It didn't happen though. I suppose for all of us involved in that period, with the so-called 'Golden Generation' tag, it will be something that we will look back on and wonder whether we could have taken England all the way.

It wasn't until September 2007 when I was asked to represent my country again; two and a half years since my last call-up to a squad and three years and three months since I'd last appeared against France in Euro 2004.

I was playing for Wigan Athletic at the time, and my team-mate Antoine Sibierski was dropping me off at home, after training. I saw a number flash up on my phone, which I didn't recognise. I answered it anyway, which I wouldn't normally do and at the other end a voice said, 'Hi Emile, it's Steve … Steve McClaren.' Anyone who knows football knows that when you receive a call like that, it's likely a prank from one of your team-mates. I went along with it. He told me he wanted me back in the England squad for a Euro 2008 qualifier at the new Wembley against Israel. It's a good job

I didn't tell him to fuck off, which I could easily have done. The longer we spoke, the more I was convinced it was him. Steve explained that he had spoken to Michael Owen about bringing me back in to play alongside him.

Michael was one of the senior players and he actually approached Steve and urged him to call me up. I was drafted into the squad after it had already been selected, as Rooney was injured and Crouchy was suspended, and Steve wanted me to start up front with Michael. I found the whole thing a bit strange, but it was great to be back. You could say it's good that Steve was willing to listen, or alternatively that it was odd that a player was influencing his team selection in that manner, but either way I became the first Wigan Athletic player to be capped for England while at the club, which was another honour.

Walking back in was different too. Rio was right when he spoke out about the fierce rivalries at club level affecting us at international level. People didn't really seem to empathise with us. I understand that, but it's hard to switch that rivalry off after being at full pump season after season. We all still got on well, but there were cliques in the group; north and south, players sitting with their club team-mates, that kind of thing. People would mix, but only on occasions. When I played for England as a Liverpool player, I would sit with my club team-mates, but now I was back as a Wigan player, I sat with the other individuals or on my own. That's just the way it was. Everyone would speak to each other, there was no issue, but it was the way it was. I didn't feel like there were cliques as such, but people would just sit with those they were closest to. A lot has been said about this by other players, but it wasn't how I felt.

I loved returning. It was like making my debut all over again. It was a real honour and a good lesson in not taking things for granted. Playing for England was something I adored doing and to pull that shirt on and walk out at Wembley, years after my last appearance, gave me real pride. I had been through a lot with England but also at club level. I was now out of the bubble of Liverpool, with all the scrutiny that comes with playing for such a gigantic club. I had the freedom to go out and enjoy my football again. I was only sad about the media reaction to my recall. I was ridiculed, almost to the point of being bullied, and I think some of the stuff that was written and said about me was uncalled for.

The media needed to realise the influence they had, and still have, over people's minds and opinions. That control almost encouraged fans to turn against me and make me a figure of fun. I gave my all for England every time. I didn't score many goals, but the way I played in my comeback made some of the media eat humble pie. I wasn't trying to prove anyone wrong. I knew what my managers, coaches and team-mates thought of my value as an individual and, more importantly, as a team player. It always came back to my goalscoring record, but the headlines were personal and

I never understood why the media didn't look at the rest of my game and speak to people who played the game. I didn't let it distract me at the time, but reading some of the stuff afterwards was eye-opening for me. It reminded me of the need to be thick-skinned as a footballer. I played in different positions in my career, fulfilling roles such as a wide man or as a provider, so it wasn't always about goals for me. I did have goals in me and scored my fair share for Leicester and Liverpool, but there's a lot more to football than just reading statistics on appearances and goals.

We beat Israel 3-0 and I was praised for my performance, but I was arguably better four days later as we beat Russia by the same scoreline. As fate would have it, I landed awkwardly on my right foot for Wigan at home to Fulham in the next game after the Russia match, and broke my fifth metatarsal. I was operated on and wouldn't be fit for at least another six weeks, meaning I would miss the qualifier away to Russia, the friendly in Austria and then the final qualifying match, at home to Croatia.

I would have been in the squad and probably starting, so I was gutted. I can remember Steve Round, one of McClaren's backroom staff, coming up to me after the Russia game I'd played in and telling me I'd had 90 per cent ball retention. He was so enthusiastic but I wasn't particularly bothered. Analysis was taking off and becoming a bigger part of the game though, and it was nice of Steve to make a point of showing me the role I'd played. People in the camp had a habit of trying to defend me or to prove to people that I was making a contribution.

When I was getting some stick at the 2002 World Cup for my lack of goals, I remember Gareth Southgate pointing out to the press that our goal against Sweden in the opening game had come from me linking up with Ashley Cole. People were always trying to evaluate my contribution. As it turned out, I only played twice for Steve McClaren, and bad fortune prevented me from linking up with Michael and helping us reach Euro 2008. After losing in Russia and then being knocked out by Croatia at Wembley, I can remember reading inquests into why we had failed, with journalists writing that if I had been fit to play, we would have qualified. That was some turnaround! A month earlier the media were giving Steve stick for picking me, now I was the saviour.

As Steve had been part of the set-up during Sven's time, we were all comfortable with him. I loved his training sessions. He was a top-class coach. I couldn't comment too much on him as a manager, as I only played those two games under him and we won them both. He will always be remembered for holding the umbrella in the rain pitchside and for being knocked out by Croatia, but there was much more to Steve than that. I got on fine with him and enjoyed working with him.

After Steve left the role, I looked at my competition as a striker and felt like I could hold my own against them; that whoever the new manager was, I could offer him something.

Crouchy was still there, but I felt there was room for me as a different option. There were others like Andy Carroll and Darren Bent coming through and, to be honest, I felt that Carlton Cole looked like he would make it, but I kept believing I would be given another chance.

That chance came under the new boss, Fabio Capello. I was picked for his first squad, for a home friendly against Switzerland in February 2008, but I missed out on playing through injury. I was then a sub for a couple of games, before making my first start under him in Croatia for a 4-1 World Cup qualifying win, which helped to exact some revenge for them knocking us out of the Euros. I scored my final two goals for England in 2009; the first in March against Slovakia in a 4-0 friendly home win and the second in June in Kazakhstan, in a qualifying victory by the same scoreline. I played in the Croatia home qualifier, a 5-1 win, which was a hugely special night and the atmosphere was electric. I had established myself as one of Capello's first-choice strikers, or at least as a first option to bring off the bench, and I was now one of the senior players in the group. That seemed to happen in the blink of an eye.

Having missed the 2006 World Cup, it was great to be part of an England squad going to a World Cup again. For that tournament to be held in South Africa was a real privilege too. Despite a lot of worries beforehand about safety issues, the tournament itself was a success. I was older, wiser and able to handle the pressures and expectations better. You just feel more familiar once you've been there and done it with England.

I was 32 by the time of that tournament. I think I had come to terms with everything by then. I wasn't bothered with what was written about me, or about what people said. I just wanted to enjoy the tournament, the experience and to try to be successful. It was my fourth major tournament and I felt like I had a different role to play; to be more responsible, to help the younger players as well. Unfortunately in training, Rio tackled me from behind and damaged his medial ligaments as I fell backwards. It was a complete accident, which everyone knew, and it happened in our first session out there. Rio had been the captain, so Steven Gerrard took over that role, Ledley King partnered John Terry in defence and Michael Dawson was called up to the squad and flew out to us as a replacement.

I was gutted for Rio. How cruel for him that moment was. We still had a strong side and decent strength in depth, but we again under performed. We drew 1-1 with the USA in our opening game, then struggled in a 0-0 draw with Algeria, before beating Slovenia 1-0 to qualify for the last 16. At the end of the Algeria game, Wayne said a few words down the camera on the pitch, live on television, about the fans booing the team. Emotions kick in at those times. No player wants to be lambasted by their own fans, so his reaction was totally understandable. The fans were entitled to let us know that it wasn't good enough as well. We worked hard that night, but we were just not at our best. That happens sometimes. We can look at tiredness, but we just didn't click. It was hugely frustrating.

Wazza, when you look back at his career, has simply been an exceptional footballer. He wears his heart on his sleeve. Too many times we try to take aspects away from players like him. We ask them to tone down the aggression, to be more disciplined. With someone like Wazza, you should just ask them how they feel, give them a pat on the back and let them go out and express themselves. He has always been a team player and is someone who gives his all. You are going to get a yellow card, a late challenge, perhaps a red from time to time, but that's part of what he is about. Let players like him play was the way I always felt. He was so strong, like a bull, and a great lad too; a real joker with a great personality. He could be quiet and thoughtful too when he wanted to be. As a player, you could see him thinking, two, maybe three steps ahead of others, such was his ability.

I started the USA and Algeria games, but was a sub against Slovenia. Defoe's goal put us through to face Germany in the last 16. Those games are always huge. It turned out to be my last-ever game for England. I was brought on in the 71st minute, when we were already 4-1 down. At 2-1, Lamps's goal wasn't given, despite crossing the line, and it may have been different but, in truth, we were light years behind them. They were better, quicker and deserved to go through. That German side was very together and had been rebuilt after a below-par period, whereas we were perhaps coming to the end of an era. It was a sad way for me to finish.

I found Fabio to be fine. He came into the job with a big reputation. Look, he was strict, he had us sticking to a regime and he was nothing like anyone I'd worked under before. He would demand that we didn't eat certain foods, like chips, pizza, butter, that kind of thing. Personally, that didn't bother me. If you are going to be an elite footballer, you don't really want to be eating that kind of food regularly anyway. It didn't go down very well with the majority of the group. You just had to deal with it and what you did in your own time was up to you. It's hard for people to accept though. We are talking about huge players, who experienced lots of success in their careers, experienced footballers being told what to eat and what not to eat. Looking back now though, I wonder if a few of the guys wonder whether they could have been more professional. Perhaps they could have committed to that regime a little more but it's easy to say that now.

Fabio was a good manager, no doubt about it, but boy could he shout. Sometimes just for the sake of it as well. You knew who was in charge when he was around. He was like the head of the army. After one long trip, we all filed in for dinner together. I had my phone out, as we'd had hours without contact with anyone. I was just scrolling through my phone, not bothering anyone and all of a sudden he went crazy at me. He picked up a lid that was keeping a dish warm and launched it on to the ground. It made a clattering noise and stopped everyone. He screamed at me for being on my phone at the table. The thing was, everyone else was doing exactly the same thing, so why had he picked me out? I nodded my head and just accepted it, as I was tired and wanted an easy life.

There was no benefit in falling out with a manager like that and you'd never win an argument with him. After all the noise and things settled down, David James turned to me and said, 'What was all that about, Emile?' while scrolling through his phone, totally oblivious. That was Jamo all over. So funny. I told him to put his phone away and chuckled to myself.

I played with some incredible players and characters for England, such as Jamo, who I'm still in touch with. In my eyes, he was physically the best goalkeeper of that era, with an incredible build. David Seaman was the best, but Jamo could have been better. I still get on very well with him, and I hope he won't mind me saying that perhaps the mental side of his game wasn't as strong as Seaman's. He's a great lad and he was unlucky not to have played more often, but the competition was fierce for that position. What a career he had though, all those years at the top. Staying awake all night to see how he would train summed him up. We had the games room at the 2002 World Cup and he'd turn to me and say, 'I bet you I'll beat you,' and before you knew it, he'd be saying, 'Best of three?' as I'd beaten him at an arcade game. He wasn't good at those games, but he wanted to take you on and be involved. I'd end up wanting to go to bed and he'd want to keep on playing all night.

Ashley Cole was the best left-back of his generation; the best in the world. He's probably England's greatest-ever player in that position. I don't feel he's received the credit he deserves either. He's had a lot of shit from the media for leaving Arsenal and for his relationships off the field. I think his decision to join Chelsea was more than justified. When you look at his career he was incredible. One thing that always amazed me was that he was a chain smoker. You'd go past his room and he'd be smoking one cigarette after another. Then he'd be on the pitch, and he'd be the fittest player out there, with Cristiano Ronaldo in his back pocket. Ashley was something else. I wasn't close to him, but I got on well with him. I didn't really have a best mate with England that I would gravitate towards to be honest. I got on well with everyone, just like I did at my clubs. I would sit on the periphery and politely join a conversation. I wasn't the kind to just jump in and start shouting the odds. That's similar to how people would be in the pub with their mates I guess though. I wasn't a forward guy, I was just me.

Rio was lively, loud and a very good sportsman. He'd win at table tennis and pool and he was a great guy to have in the group for the general mood. You need someone to pick people up and he was like that. He was a leader, but then there were captains throughout that era: Becks, Gerrard, Terry, Rio, Sol, Carra all of them. I also got on well with John Terry. I didn't know him as long as I knew some of the other guys, but I probably spent more time and had more conversations with JT than the rest of them. When the racism allegations against him came out, I found it all a bit weird, as I'd not only got on with him, but I had never had any reason to think anything like that about him. It all happened after I stopped playing for England, so I didn't see first-hand what things were like, but the incident obviously led to Capello leaving as well, and would have made John and Rio's relationship very difficult given that the incident involved Anton, Rio's brother.

Sol was different. I like to keep myself to myself but Sol took that to another level. He loves to be alone. As a group we would pop out at tournaments for a coffee when we could. We'd get there and Sol would already be there, just sitting on his own. That's fine in itself, but then he wouldn't really make a move to sit with anyone, or invite you over. He'd just stay there on his own without saying a word to anyone. It happened a few times.

He was a fantastic defender, so tough and a true leader on the pitch, so I'm not surprised he's gone into management given his leadership skills. I don't like the way he's been treated by the game. He put numerous applications in for jobs, and in some cases didn't even get a reply. He's one of the most decorated defenders in the game, and I don't like the piss-taking he's had to put up with on social media, with people laughing at him. There should be more respect. Yes, he's unique, he's a character, he doesn't conform to the norms of society, but so what. He's a good guy and we should celebrate people like Sol, not deride them.

Lamps was someone I'd played with since youth level with England, and even then he was a real talent who stood out above others. No one shoots at goal more than Lamps, and he's scored some remarkable goals and big, important goals too in his career. Strangely, I never really got to know him very well. He grew up with some of the others, but I was in the Midlands so I didn't know them or play with them as a kid. I would be with Lamps and the others for a few days and then back to my club when I was with the England youth sides. I didn't socialise with any of them. I did the socialising at Leicester as a young lad with the experienced guys and then later at Aston Villa, as I was older we could perhaps go out for meals as couples. With England, I didn't have that time.

I remember Owen Hargreaves coming into the squad and all I knew about him was that he played for Bayern Munich, so I thought he must be good. And he was. Owen could be very to the point, blunt, a little abrupt at times. We would be talking about a player, perhaps an opponent, and Owen would, out of nowhere, just say, 'Nah, he's crap. He's not good enough.' I guess that's why he's made a decent career as a pundit. That honesty will serve him well on television. He was honest with his managers as well, when analysing his own players. As lads who have grown up in England, we never said anything like that. We were always so reserved and polite, so that was different, but again, I liked Owen.

I can't not write about Joe Cole too. He was amazing. What a player. Joe came into the England squad as a young lad, having done very well for West Ham United. I found it fascinating to watch him train. We were doing a simple drill, just passing, crossing and finishing. Joe had to complicate the drill, probably just to stimulate and challenge himself, so he did a rabona half-volley, into the path of someone to score. It was a real stand-out moment that I'll always remember. I was shocked at his quality and his technical ability, aligned with his confidence to do that when he was so young and surrounded by the best players in the country. Nothing seemed to faze him. I was saddened that some of that natural flair and skill was, shall we say, knocked out of him by managers who wanted him to track back and do other work. I would just let Joe be Joe. We were begging for the next Gazza and Joe could have been that.

I think during the Sven era we had too much talent in the midfield. We didn't have the balance. We had too many good players to fit in. Lamps and Gerrard were often given the nod in the middle, with Becks on the right and then Scholesy and Joe would fill in on the left. Other countries like Italy, Germany, France or Brazil, seemed to just pick the best squad and then the best-balanced team. It's difficult when you have that talent to decide upon, but that's where the managers earn their money. We were always a little bit imbalanced on the left. Maybe if we'd have worked that out, we'd have won something. Player for player, we had one of the best sides in the world, but we didn't quite get the team balance right.

I have no regrets about my time with England. I loved all of it. Every time we walked out, the opponents wanted to beat us desperately. No matter the team you were playing, there's always a history with us, which made it that little bit harder. I wish we'd won something, of course. I know I dealt with the strains of it all better as I got older. I would have loved that experience, that knowledge of it all at the start, but that's not the way it works. Mentally, football can take you to a bad place sometimes. It's so tough. If you're in a good place, you can play out of your skin. Playing for England was a dream though, so I have no complaints.

So I only scored seven goals for England. It's seven more than most people get to score; and one of those came in the World Cup, with another in a 5-1 win against Germany. I'm laughing as I write this though, as I don't need to defend myself. I'm comfortable with what I achieved. I targeted playing 50 games for England. I thought that would really be something. I reached 62 in the end. I played in two World Cups and two European Championships too. If I'd have been offered that as a teenager, I would have snapped your hand off. I honestly think, and I don't want this to sound bitter, but people don't remember any of that when they think of me. They just think of what the media have said about me.

I had the chance to do what people would give anything for: to play alongside the best players, for great managers and to travel the world representing my country. It's something that I often think of and is something that no one can ever take away from me. I lived the dream.

CHAPTER NINE

Out of the Bubble ...
in to Birmingham

I ALWAYS envisaged that I would move back home to Leicester, or at least closer to home, so when I signed for Birmingham and lived initially in the city centre and then moved to Meriden, I thought I would be happy there; close to a big city and my work, near to my family in Leicester. I thought I would end up back in Leicester one day too and bring my family up there. It's funny how things change though. I felt like I belonged in the North West, which, when you think about how I was at Liverpool at the start, in tears and feeling alone, is some turnaround. I couldn't wait to get started at Blues though. I was buzzing to be playing for another club, and to face another challenge.

Liverpool was huge, and with all respect to Birmingham, it's a completely different sized club. That meant there was an onus on me to deliver with goals and performances; a different kind of pressure. At Liverpool, the standards were so high that if you didn't perform, you would be dropped without a second thought. At Birmingham, people were now looking towards me as the main signing, the guy to turn to if we needed something to happen. It was similar to how I felt at Leicester at the start of my career.

Steve Bruce was great. He came to my house, made me feel welcome and offered to support me in whatever way he could. I appreciated that. He'd showed huge faith in me, paying around £6m to bring me to the club, so he'd banked a lot on me being a success. The facilities were similar to Leicester and it turned out to be a breath of fresh air for me. I was away from the scrutiny of Liverpool and that relentless pressure, day after day. I felt good. I was free of the chains and able to get back to expressing myself. There was no magnifying glass on me anymore. No one was interested in me. I felt like the way that Birmingham played would suit my own style and my agent, Struan, wanted to protect me and spoke about the risks of them going down in my first season, making sure I knew what I was agreeing to. I was adamant that we wouldn't. I hadn't joined a club, expecting to be in any kind of relegation battle. I was so confident I could help Blues and improve them.

I loved seeing some familiar faces too. Sav was already at the club and then Muzzy signed from Leicester soon after I did. It was like a mini-reunion for us. I felt sure I would have linked up well with Muzzy, but he had a nightmare with injuries at Blues. The fans never saw what he was about. It was such a shame. Birmingham fans would have loved him, but it wasn't to be for him. It was desperately unfair.

We also signed Mario Melchiot, who was a big character. I'd had some fierce battles with him while I was at Liverpool and he was playing for Chelsea. Mario became a good friend and we are still in touch to this day. He's a lively guy and great to be around. He is a true leader and was someone who always took control of situations. What I admired a lot about Mario was that he would give time to younger players, to advise them. That was important to me too and stood him out from others.

A signing who came with big expectations but never really worked out was another Chelsea man, Jesper Gronkjaer. I would watch him in training and think at times that there didn't seem to be too much to him, but he was so quick and all of a sudden he would make something happen. He was a talent, but for whatever reason he just didn't suit Birmingham and by the January of my first season, within months of joining, he had left.

I had to change my game at Blues. I was used to having Gerrard, Danny Murphy, Gary Mac, or Litmanen threading balls through to me. Again, with respect, I was going to have to adapt. Players have to do that. They have to get used to different quality and styles at new clubs. Don't get me wrong, Birmingham had quality players, but Liverpool were world class.

We added some experience through Darren Anderton and Dwight Yorke. I had played a little in the national squad with Darren; a great passer, superb crosser, but he had suffered with injuries and by the time we had him I think his legs were going. He was very unlucky throughout his career, as he achieved a great deal but also missed so much. Dwight was coming towards the end of his career as well, but he was still very strong and was super fit. He had a lot to give back to younger players and to myself too, so I enjoyed learning from him and working with him. Even to train next to Dwight was a real honour. Julian Gray came in from Crystal Palace too and he was a good signing by Bruce, added to what was a stable, decent squad.

I felt like the fans were excited to see me play and they backed me from day one. You arrive with a reputation; the goal against Germany, the trophies for Leicester and Liverpool: and that helps, but you still have to deliver. There's no relying on past achievements. It's sink or swim time. I'm really humbled by the fact that whenever I go back to Birmingham today, I am welcomed by the fans. Even if I wasn't always at my best, fans recognise players who graft and I always gave my all for them.

I scored my first goal in a 1-0 home win over Manchester City, which was our first win of the season too, and we continued in that manner, seemingly comfortable in mid-table. In January, Steve brought another influx of players in. Jermaine Pennant was probably the most notorious of those additions. Look, everyone got on well with him, but he was just a bit weird. He was different. I know he's been on reality shows and chat shows and has revealed a lot about the things he did in his career. He was, in my experience, great when you had a one-on-one conversation with him, but he was an entertainer and so disorganised as a person.

I felt for him. He'd turn up late for training, and he'd have pieces of toast just tucked down his socks. We'd be out on the field playing and if he didn't have the ball, he'd be bending down to take the toast out and eat it. I would be shaking my head. That wasn't professional and it was just strange. I can remember the gaffer putting him in a quiet place, an apartment near to Solihull, and he smuggled himself out of there to an apartment in the city centre and ran wild.

I can see why Steve signed him though. Put Jermaine on a football field and his ability was clear for all to see. He was exciting, a great crosser with pace and skills, but mentally, he wasn't focused or stable. I'm not sure that the fame or money changed him though; I think he would have been that way regardless of all the noise around him. He craved the attention, perhaps a little like Dioufy did at Liverpool, and Jermaine ended up playing for Liverpool a year later. I remember him playing for us with an ankle tag on, having to get special permission to play in night games [following a drink-drive conviction]. He could have played for England regularly, but instead he was eating pizzas every single day. He'd add extra cheese and not care. He did it every day, whereas it should have been a treat. That shows just how important discipline and focus is within football. You can have all the ability in the world, but if you aren't stable and settled, you may never actually be present enough to perform.

Steve had a lot of pressure on him to manage Jermaine's character as he'd stuck his neck out to sign him from Arsenal. It was on his head to make that work, but Jermaine was a grown adult so how much can you actually do? He was a good man-manager, Steve, and had strong motivational skills. We knocked heads a lot at the beginning. You have to get used to each other. He demanded more from me, and I felt as if I was giving my all. He knew that I had to score goals and be a provider for the amount he'd invested in me. Football management is a draining, all-consuming job. You are the head of a family and the buck stops with you.

Steve had plenty on his plate and I didn't want to cause him any extra problems. I decided to stop arguing with him. I got my head down and if he pushed me on something I would just say, 'Yes boss,' and the disagreement would be over. I found that was an easier way of dealing with him. You weren't going to win an argument and the shouting didn't do anyone any good. I was good at doing that in my career. Just listen, nod your head, step back from confrontation and let things pass. It was my way of coping with it. Steve was a shouter, a ranter, but he didn't really swear at me as such. He didn't make it personal. He had a good coaching staff around him and he was a winner as a player, so he demanded the best from you. I think he tried to keep things simple. He didn't want to complicate the way we played and that was important. He kept his messages clear and the players responded to him.

Salif Diao came in on loan from Liverpool to help solidify our midfield, especially given Muzzy's injury. Perhaps we were too direct for Salif, as he liked to get the ball down and play. Sav left us in January too and joined Blackburn. He's since admitted that he forced that move through. At the time he said it was to be nearer to his family home in Wrexham, but Birmingham is actually nearer than Blackburn. He just wanted the move, despite having signed a new contract at Blues. It was a loss for us, as Robbie was an effective player and worked very hard, so we missed his industry.

Walter Pandiani, a Uruguayan striker, joined us on loan and had a positive impact in that initial spell. He played alongside me and came with a big reputation from the Spanish league, where he had scored a lot of goals for Deportivo de La Coruna. He was technically a good player, and I think the gaffer felt that playing him alongside me would see us as an aerial threat, with Jermaine supplying the assists. Walter was great in the air, but it didn't really work out for him in England. We signed a lot of players during my time at Birmingham, but Steve managed to blend the team together well into what was essentially a direct style of play. Despite the signings, I always had the feeling that we were punching above our weight, and that eventually caught up with us in my second season.

We were a workmanlike outfit. The backbone of the team were regulars like Maik Taylor in goal, Kenny Cunningham, Matthew Upson and Jamie Clapham in defence, Stephen Clemence and Damien Johnson in midfield, Stan Lazardis as a wide option and Clinton Morrison up front as an option along with me and the others I've mentioned. They were good players, all of them, but they weren't stars. The team was built in the mould of the gaffer; strong, reliable, hard working, hard to beat, full of effort and desire. David Dunn was another player who had the ability to show flair and unlock defences, but like Muzzy and Anderton, he was injured and meant we missed another quality option.

Whose fault was all of these injuries? Were they just down to bad luck? The individuals themselves? Or the training? We could have had an all-star side of big names, but they were never available at the same time. Clem was one of the reliable ones and he has since gone on to work with the gaffer as part of his coaching staff. I go back a long way with him; back to our England youth days, so it was quite a journey we had both been on before being reunited. He is a very knowledgeable guy and had a good footballing brain, so I'm not surprised that he's stayed in the game.

We enjoyed some great results in that 2004/05 season; winning 1-0 at Liverpool in November, beating Villa 2-1 away in December, and I had a good run of form around that time, scoring in four consecutive games against West Bromwich Albion, Middlesbrough, Fulham and Newcastle United.

In February we completed the double over Liverpool with a 2-0 home win and did the same against Villa a month later. I managed to open the scoring in that game, with a shot from a tight angle, which the Dane Thomas Sorensen allowed to squirm under his body. I scored against him in the 2002 World Cup, so I obviously liked playing against him. I exploded with relief after the goal. I'd played in big derby games before and this was another one. It was all the fans talked about, and for us to play our part in completing a double over Villa was pretty special.

It was a crazy game. The atmosphere was fiery and the hatred from both sets of fans was strong. They were a good side: Lee Hendrie, Darius Vassell, Nobby Solano, Gareth Barry, Olaf Mellberg, they had talent all the way through. Julian Gray got the second to make it a comfortable finish. So much so that Mario decided to start doing some tricks on the pitch. He was doing kick-ups and flicked the ball over a Villa player and collected it the other side of him. The crowd responded and were shouting 'Ole!' on each touch of the ball. We weren't directly rubbing it in their faces, but it had the same effect. Mario was very skilful for a defender, given his Dutch background and having played lots of small-sided possession football.

Hendrie wasn't having any of it and reacted to Mario. Lee was at him, shouting and pointing at him. Lee is a big Villa fan and was a big player for them and he was hurting. He obviously felt that Mario had been disrespectful. Mario is a calm guy and he kept telling Lee to leave him alone. We've reached the tunnel by this time with the fans goading the Villa players and cheering us. Once more, considering that I was a pretty placid player, I lost it as Lee wouldn't leave Mario alone. I've gone hurtling over and pushed him out of the way.

All hell broke loose, just like in Turkey with England. Stefan Postma, the Villa reserve goalkeeper, ran over and grabbed me around the neck, which I wriggled out of and then we were all rolling around, punches being thrown all over the place. It was mad. Mario apologised afterwards in interviews for his showboating, which was good of him to do, but technically he did nothing wrong. He was just entertaining the fans and enjoying the win. The FA ended up investigating the whole thing. I think Villa would have done the same as Mario did if it was the other way around.

In the final game of the season, we hosted Arsenal and beat them 2-1. I got the winner in the last minute after Dennis Bergkamp had equalised just moments before. We finished in 12th place and I can honestly be proud of my own season, finishing as top scorer with 11 goals, and being named as the supporters' and players' player of the season. I had delivered and as a team we had preserved our top-flight status. You never know how well you are going to settle, and if you had offered me that when I signed, I would have been happy. I had enjoyed the extra responsibility. Okay, so we didn't create as many chances as at Liverpool, but that meant I had to finish the chances I did get.

We didn't follow this up though. In football, I always looked at my previous season and how I could improve, how I could help the team and how we could finish higher and exceed our aims. The 2005/06 season was a disaster as we did none of that. Our signings didn't really light things up. They did okay, but we weren't the same side. Darren Carter, Robbie Blake, Anderton and Morrison left, and we brought Walter in permanently as well as Mehdi Nafti, who had also been with us on loan, and signed Mikael Forssell, as well as Jiri Jarosik and Nicky Butt on loan.

I'd played with Nicky in the 2002 World Cup, when Pelé named him in the team of the tournament. Butty was a big name and a very good player, coming into a difficult situation later in his career. The challenge he was facing was very different to what he was used to at Manchester United. Mikael came in with a reputation too, following his time at Chelsea. He was hard working and was an exceptional talent, but I felt he was soft mentally, which I would put down to his injury record over the years. As soon as he felt something, he wouldn't play. He'd had bad luck with injuries, so I understood why he was so wary of doing damage again. He had superb football intelligence, but it was sad to see the effect that injuries had on him. I've seen so many players suffer mentally from the weight of injuries, but also struggle to manage the pressures of being a professional footballer.

I didn't really know what position Jiri was best in, but he was a very good player. We played him out wide and he wasn't really someone who was going to go burning past players. I liked him playing more centrally, but we needed legs in there. I'm not sure he fitted into our plans, the style of play, and again, the situation we faced. I never really contemplated that we would be in a relegation dogfight that season. I expected us to reach mid-table again and be comfortable. We had two cup runs as well, reaching the quarter-finals in both the FA Cup and the League Cup, and that probably took its toll on the squad. We perhaps didn't have the strength in depth required for a relegation battle and those extra games.

I started the season well with a couple of goals against West Brom in a 3-2 win in August and we held Liverpool to a 2-2 draw at home a month later. However, we lost to Villa at home in October and I scored in 2-1 home defeat to West Ham United in December. My other goals came against Sunderland in a 1-0 home win in February and in a 2-2 draw with Millwall in the League Cup. I played 40 games and only scored five goals that season. Those 11 goals I scored the previous year were crucial and the team missed them. The onus was on me and I didn't deliver what I wanted. I found it hard. I never gave up trying, but we were not the same side.

In the January, we let Walter leave as he'd struggled for goals and the gaffer brought Chris Sutton and DJ Campbell in. DJ had scored goals at a lower level and in the FA Cup and had pace, whereas Chris was a senior pro with the experience to help us. We weren't playing attractive stuff though, and it was a difficult time for anyone to come in. It's so hard to turn the tide when you are staring relegation in the face.

We exited the FA Cup with an awful 7-0 home defeat to Liverpool in front of a packed stadium. I didn't play that night. What can you say about a result like that? The cup runs were meant to give us confidence, to help inspire a winning mentality, but this was shattering to our confidence.

We finished in 18th place, just four points behind Portsmouth and eight points behind Villa. We were just short of a couple of players, a couple of wins, but ultimately we were relegated from the Premier League. That was an awful feeling. It was one of the worst of my career. It was devastating for the fans, but the players felt it as well.

I don't think I did any worse in terms of my effort and my performances, but I didn't get the goals I wanted. It was a strange season. I was used to success with Leicester and Liverpool, winning promotion, cups and playing for England. I'd never experienced relegation as a regular player. I felt hollow. It all came down to mentality for me. Even though we were punching above our weight a little, if we'd have shown some character, we wouldn't have gone down. At Leicester, we had the big characters like Walshy, Lennon and Elliott who would have dragged us out of it. We as players have to take responsibility for that failure at Birmingham. When you're at a smaller club, not a Liverpool where you expect to win every game, you have to create the mentality. It's not already there. Some games, certain players will go into the match hoping for a small loss. That's wrong, but it happens. How do you change the attitude to a positive when you are losing games every week as well? That's where a manager earns his money, and gives the players the belief in their own ability and in his methods.

I look back with real fondness at my time at Birmingham though. I really loved my time there. It was a turning point in my career and in my life. It gave me the buzz for football again. In essence, I didn't want to leave Liverpool, but I needed to leave them. If I'd have stayed, I don't know if I'd have been the same person. I was scrutinised for the clothes I wore, what I did, even how my hair and stubble was, whether I had an earring or not. When I signed for the club I turned up wearing Puma sportswear, and should have been wearing a suit. No one had told me. I was criticised in the media, with comments made about the way I looked. If I'd have stayed at Liverpool, the life would have been drained from me from the pressure. My mood would have been different. It affected my lifestyle, my health, everything.

* * *

Birmingham put a smile back on my face, despite the sad finish to my time there. I'm grateful to Steve for putting his faith in me and for giving me the opportunity to play for a great club, and I'm thankful to the fans. They were great with me throughout, and win, lose or draw they never battered us. Even with the relegation, they still supported us. They deserve great credit for that. I still see Blues fans today at events, and they have complimentary things to say. That means a lot to me.

If I'm honest, there was never a thought of me staying once we were relegated. I wanted to play in the Premier League. It was as simple as that. Wigan Athletic came straight in for me and like two years earlier with Blues, the move was very straightforward. Wigan was a similar set-up to Blues; a working-class club and it suited me. There were no other clubs interested as the move happened so quickly. It felt comfortable for me as I was staying in the top flight and I would be back in the North West. I didn't like to mess around. Wigan made it clear that they wanted me. I liked the fact that despite being relegated and only scoring five goals that season, I was wanted. I guess my reputation helped and they would have thought that I was within their reach as Blues had gone down. It was a good move for all parties as Blues managed to get a decent fee for me too and they were fine with me speaking to Wigan.

I was disappointed that I hadn't played for England while at Birmingham, especially in the first season where I was playing well, but then not having that additional pressure probably helped me. To play for England means you have to be on top of your game at all times. You can't have a blip. That period was still part of the 'Golden Generation', and the 2006 World Cup had such media coverage with the WAGs [wives and girlfriends] in Germany. I didn't personally feel they were doing anything wrong. Young women, on holiday, having a drink and partying. Isn't that what people do when they go away? The media, who followed them around, taking photos and providing tabloid scoops were the ones I would be questioning. It was a relief to not be caught up in any of that.

Wigan had a small squad, but they were hard workers and I was used to that now. I knew the challenge would be difficult as they didn't have the spending power of the bigger clubs, but I was excited about it. I was in a good place, loving my football and I couldn't wait for another adventure.

CHAPTER TEN

Fighting for Our Lives

WIGAN were a club on the up when I joined them. They were similar to Birmingham and had established themselves in the Premier League. Dave Whelan had spent a bit of money and as an unknown package they had shocked a few of the bigger clubs. I'd found them tough to play against and I felt like they were an exciting team, with great potential.

I couldn't wait to join up with my new team-mates. After the disappointment of relegation with Blues, I needed some positivity. The manager, Paul Jewell, felt that I was a typical number nine and needed me to play that role. That was what pretty much all of my managers said to me though, so it was nothing new. He wanted me to lead the line, hold the ball up, bring others into play and score some goals. I felt that Wigan's style suited me. They wanted to attack and could mix it up between playing a bit and going direct, both of which I was used to.

Jewell was a typical British football manager; I found him to be loud, a motivator who wouldn't hold back from shouting or tearing a strip off you. He was funny, with that infamous Scouse wit and he got us going for each game. He helped create a great environment too. We didn't have the biggest of squads and at that size of club, it's difficult to turn things around when you're on a losing run, but Paul got the best out of us and he pushed us right until the end. The biggest challenge for him was to get the group to believe in themselves, even when form was poor, but his man-management skills came through.

We bought a few players that summer including Chris Kirkland, Fitz Hall, Denny Landzaat, Kevin Kilbane and David Cotterill. Cotts had a lot of pressure on him. He was just a kid and came in with a big reputation from his time at Bristol City and a £2m price tag hanging over him. I felt that he, like many, many young players became a little trapped in the football bubble and mentality, buying fast cars and spending money. I don't think the fast car fitted with the club and certainly not with the gaffer, who wasn't impressed either. I think his missus had 'WAG' on her number plate too.

It's hard for young lads having money thrown at them and not being advised correctly. There are countless lads who did this and then late on in their careers they regretted it. It was tough for Cotts to settle in and he never really got the opportunities he would have liked at Wigan.

'Killer' Kilbane had a great work ethic and mentality on the pitch and was so supportive of the younger lads off the pitch. He and goalkeeper Mike Pollitt were as thick as thieves. They were always joking, but that was great for the environment. The lads absolutely loved coming in to training as it was so much fun around the place. They contributed towards that massively. Everyone enjoyed working together. There was a huge unity. Probably not quite like I had at Leicester, but that was unique.

There were key characters already at the club, who helped to form the backbone of the side. Paul Scharner was very good, but he was a strange lad. He had a mental coach who would visit him and work with him. Paul would do things to stand out, I think. He'd train with you one day and then the next day at a game, he'd have a hat on, take it off and reveal a quirky, dyed haircut. It was about his persona. He played at centre-back and in midfield and scored goals. He was aggressive, very tough in the tackle and strong in the air. He was great for us, but I couldn't quite get my head around the haircut and the mental coach.

Antonio Valencia was just so powerful. He was young, joined from Villareal, knew no English and just got on with his football. He was at the club for three years before joining Manchester United, but when I left, he still didn't speak English. At an awards night, he was up on stage accepting an honour and his speech was straight to the point, 'Wigan … goo. Fans … goo.' I didn't want to take the piss, but after that long at the club, you'd have thought he would have known a little more and at least how to say the word 'good'. There were other Spanish speakers at Wigan though, so he didn't need to know, I guess. He played some incredible football for us though.

Emmerson Boyce went on to become a club legend. He typified Wigan. He never gave up and was so reliable, staying for over ten years. Emmerson was usually the first name on the team sheet. A real rock. Leighton Baines was some player too. When I joined, I was surprised he was that good and that Wigan had him. Everton let him go as he was deemed too small, but they took him back and the rest is history.

I scored on my home debut, a 1-0 win over Reading, and then got goals against Blackburn, Manchester City, two against Chelsea, another at Reading, and then against Bolton, Villa and Spurs. In October and November, we had a four-match winning run, before things fell apart and we lost eight games on the bounce in December and January. That's what I mean when I say that you can struggle to turn things around at the highest level. It's an unforgiving standard. The gaffer brought David Unsworth in from Sheffield United, and little did we know how crucial he would be at the end of the season. David was experienced and that's what we needed. When heads are down, you need people like that to step up and help the younger lads through.

On the final day of the season we were left with a straightforward equation, but not an easy task. We had to go to Bramall Lane and win against Sheffield United to stay up. Sheffield United also needed a draw or West Ham United to lose at Old Trafford to remain in the division. We had been on a slippery slope up to that point. I never felt like we would go down, and after every defeat I felt like we would win the next one and then the one after that, but we didn't. The tension built to that final day. I knew that people were looking at me to drag us out of the mess. I did everything I could. I was the big summer signing and I felt like I'd pulled my weight, but we were still faced with that stressful final day. I played up front with Lee McCulloch and we battered them, although they created the better chances.

It was an epic game. Absolutely unbelievable. The raw emotion of the day was so much for everyone to handle. We took the lead through Scharner early on, but a few minutes before half time Jon Stead equalised for them. That's all they needed to relegate us. The atmosphere was incredible. There was a long delay for that goal as Stead and Pollitt were injured, as was Ryan Taylor for us who went off injured. We'd already lost Arjan de Zeeuw through injury too.

It looked like we would go in level at the break and regroup until Phil Jagielka handled the ball for no reason and we had a penalty. Up stepped Unsworth who had just come on for the injury. He hammered the penalty home and we were 2-1 up. We had chances, but so did they in the second half. I gave the ball away which left Danny Webber through on goal, but his shot hit the post and somehow stayed out. I've never been so relieved in my life. I also nearly extended our lead with an overhead volley, but Paddy Kenny pulled off a great save.

McCulloch was sent off with 16 minutes remaining and we were down to the bare bones, which resulted in Caleb Folan coming on up front and me reverting to centre-back for the remainder of the game. It was all hands to the pump. Stead came close again. The tension was unbearable. It was absolutely frantic. West Ham won away to Manchester United, with Carlos Tevez and Javier Mascherano playing for them towards the end of that season in controversial circumstances, so the Blades threw everything at us.

It felt like I was heading balls out of the box for hours, when in reality it was just 15 minutes or so. I leant on all those Friday training sessions at Leicester of Young versus Old, where I had Walshy, Taggs, Matty and Marshy just heading everything and pushing me down. Those boys would have been proud of me that day. I just headed the ball and when it was low I kicked it as far as I could. I never once looked for a team-mate. We were being bombarded and I was just hacking it back where it came from. I'd never played as a centre-back in my professional career, but it was great fun. I loved the challenge and it's a game I'll never forget. When the final whistle blew the overriding feeling was one of relief.

Sadly, the relief didn't last long. We were all sitting in the dressing room afterwards and the gaffer said he would see us all on Tuesday. You could see how stressed he was. He had taken on all of our worries, the feelings of the whole club and he looked like he was carrying the weight of the world on his shoulders. We were expecting that we'd be off for the summer now, so people weren't happy that we had to come back in. I could see that something was wrong though. It was such a draining season for everyone. Football has a way of consuming you, so you can't control yourself. It's like a drug that just consumes you. I've experienced it many times. It was clear that the gaffer had gone past the point of no return.

We showed up to the training ground on the Tuesday and I think we all knew what was coming. That season had sapped the life and the energy out of the gaffer. He announced that he would be resigning to take a break from the game. He'd done such a fantastic job for Wigan and people understood that he had a life away from football. In general, being a football manager is not good for your health and probably not good for your personal life. That game against Sheffield United was essentially like a play-off final. It must have been heartbreaking for them to lose at home to us, and to see us celebrating, with our winning goal scored by a player we signed directly from them.

I had a good relationship with the gaffer. Paul was fine. I never had a problem with him. I scored eight goals in 38 games and I gave my all that season. It was a tough campaign and it was all about survival. It's strange, because we didn't win anything but it's a season and a final game that the fans will still talk about today. You could call it celebrating mediocrity, but we were right to celebrate keeping Wigan in the top flight.

That was a great achievement, against all the odds. It was like winning a trophy; a special moment in my life.

For the 2007/08 season Chris Hutchings took over as manager, having been Paul's assistant prior to that. We started really well, with two wins from the first three games, but we soon fell into bad form and Chris left in November, with us stuck in the relegation zone. The difficult thing for Chris was the transition from coach to manager. Chris was a very good coach and I enjoyed his training. I'm not saying he couldn't have been a good manager too, but once you've done that role, it's tough to convince everyone that you can be the main man. As players, we are used to them being in one role and the relationship is different. It is slowly changing now with the introduction of head coaches and sporting directors, but back then it was a huge leap. Frank Barlow took over as caretaker and then a familiar face for me was back as my manager; Steve Bruce.

Unfortunately, I broke my foot in the Fulham game, meaning I missed England duty but wasn't available for the new gaffer as well. He wasn't the only familiar face I was working with either. Mario Melchiot came in, who I'd been with at Birmingham. He was playing abroad and called me to ask me what Wigan was like. I convinced him that the set-up was like Blues and that he would enjoy the club, the fans and living in the area. He was a great addition and, just as he had been at Blues, he was great to have around the place, boosting everyone's mood.

I felt like we were building a sustainable Premier League side and Bruce helped with that development. We had Antoine Sibierski, who was technically one of the best players I've played with. That might surprise people, but he was fantastic with the ball at his feet. I always remember him speaking about his past in France and loving the game out there, but preferring to play in England. There was just one thing he couldn't get used to though; the tackling. In France, if someone came near him, he would hit the ground and get a free kick, yet in England he could be put on his backside and it was deemed a fair challenge. The pace and the intensity was quite an adjustment for him. He also commented on how if you were 2-0 up with 20 minutes to go, teams would take it easy and the game would just fizzle out. Here, if you were 2-0 down on 90 minutes, you were still expected to push right until the final whistle. He loved that. He could strike a ball beautifully, from a standing position, or on the volley, he was genuine quality.

Titus Bramble was a key player for us. He had a reputation for making glaring errors. He was highly rated as a young defender and had commanded big transfer fees, but the media and the public just honed in on those errors. On his day, Titus could have been as good as any English defender, I mean that, he had everything, but he also had one big mistake in him per game. I don't know why that was, but if you looked at his ability on the ball, to spray passes out, left and right foot, his strength, tackling and heading, he was right up there, but the mistakes cost him taking his game to the next level.

It never became a mental issue for him though, as he was able to brush the scrutiny off. People expected him to make a mistake, that's what he was known for, but if you looked at his game as a whole he was very, very good.

Marcus Bent joined us and had a successful spell at the club. We had played together at England youth level at the Toulon Tournament. He had great stature, finished as our top scorer that season, and was very quick. He worked well with me. Even though we could be quite similar, he took some of the workload off me, which meant we had other options instead of just looking for me every time. He would run the channels well, but equally he could hold the ball up and keep opponents at arm's length. I know he's had a lot of troubles since finishing playing, but I'm sure a lot of players have suffered too. While we are playing, the game itself and the money can mask a lot of issues, but once you are retired, unless you find something to do, those issues can rear their head.

As I didn't depart Birmingham on bad terms, I was pleased to be working with Steve again. I liked the way he played and I got on well with him. Nothing changed at Wigan for me. We still got on fine. I was pleased that he appreciated the contribution I made, and I knew what I had to do to keep him happy; work hard and try to get goals or set others up.

I grabbed a couple of goals in April against Chelsea and Spurs to nudge us towards safety and we ended up finishing 14th with me scoring four goals in 29 games, in a season which was interrupted by injuries. When I broke my foot against Fulham, I was convinced I could carry on playing and tried to run it off without knowing to what extent I had damaged myself.

I had to stop, take my boot off and my foot blew up in size. I couldn't get my boot back on, so there was no way I was playing, and before I knew it I had crutches under my arms. I had to have a screw put in and I still have that in my foot today. It was probably the worst injury of my career, apart from maybe a cartilage issue I had later in my career, but I was fortunate to avoid broken legs or ACLs. It was just the timing; ruling me out of the crucial Euro 2008 qualifiers and missing out on eight or nine Premier League games. The effect it had lasted as well. I was on a huge roll with confidence, likewise with my England displays against Israel and Russia, but when I came back I just wasn't the same. I couldn't run properly. My equilibrium was totally out of sync. I didn't feel right for weeks, maybe months. It's such a frustration for players.

My final season at Wigan was the 2008/09 campaign. In the summer, the gaffer brought in Lee Cattermole. I think Lee could have possibly been an England midfield regular, maybe even a captain if he'd reached his potential. He was a born leader, a real fighter, who could play a bit too. To be honest though, I think he became unreliable, in the sense that you knew he was a walking risk for a yellow card. I think people forget what a good player he has been in his career, but the yellow cards, and sometimes reds, are what people first think of with Catts.

Brucey brought Olivier Kapo in; another player with a big reputation. If I am honest, he seemed as if he was more bothered about his lifestyle than his football. He had great ability, but he didn't do as well for us as he should have done. We needed workers but he was, shall we say, more of a leisured footballer. Amr Zaki came in and, I'm going to be honest here, if you'd have seen him playing in his first training session, you'd have thought someone had taken a payment for letting him play. He was terrible. He couldn't control the ball. His training didn't really improve, but put him out on the pitch in a game and at times he was unplayable. He would score acrobatic goals and I couldn't believe it. I came from a place where you trained how you played. That was always my approach, so I couldn't work out why some players were so different in terms of their effort and their end product.

* * *

I scored in a 5-0 win at Hull City, and a 2-1 win at Portsmouth in November, which was my 100th top-flight goal. I didn't know until afterwards. It was never something I was too focused on as I would take each game and each goal as they came. It had been pissing it down, so I used the greasy surface to allow the ball to roll past me, drawing Sol Campbell in and I slid the ball home past David James. I was very proud to join such an elite club of players. I was known as a provider of goals, but this proved I could finish too. I was asked after the game whether the 100 goals meant more to me, or the three points on the day and I felt like I should be honest; it was the 100 goals, no doubt about it.

My last goal for Wigan came a month later against Blackburn in a 3-0 win. In January there was some speculation about my future. There were even articles linking me with a return to Liverpool. I didn't know anything about it, so my agent made some enquiries but there didn't seem to be any truth to the rumours. Brucey spoke out about the speculation and said that Wigan was the right place for me to be, to continue my England ambitions.

I've never really spoken about this, but I was more than happy to sign a new deal with Wigan and commit to them for longer. My deal would run out in the summer, but I was happy to stay beyond that. The truth is, Wigan didn't offer me a deal. Nothing materialised, so I had to look elsewhere. Aston Villa came in for me that month, with Martin O'Neill their manager at the time, and I was keen on the move. Everything was agreed and then Wigan made a gesture towards keeping me, but it was too late by then. Everyone knew I was happy at Wigan and that I would have stayed. I guess they were looking to cash in on me and Villa paid £3.5m. That probably made sense for them and there was no turning back for me.

Martin had followed my career and I loved playing for him, as most players did. I was still fit and healthy. We trained very well at Wigan and I noticed that my fitness levels were really high, so I must credit the staff there for that. It was probably all the chasing down of defenders that I had to do within the system we played. Brucey would moan at me for overdoing it sometimes. I picked up an ankle knock once for chasing back too much and catching a kick off someone. I was doing what he'd told me to do, but this time I'd picked up an injury. I suppose his anger with me showed how much he valued me, which was an indirect compliment.

Villa were trying to break into the top four, and were on the up, playing very free-flowing, attack-minded football. They had some seriously good players under the gaffer as well. I always believed I could play for another side like Villa, and I had re-established myself in the England side, so I had confidence and belief in myself. I had just turned 31, so all I can think is that Wigan took the cash and moved me on as they felt I'd seen better days, but I didn't feel that old.

I loved my time at Wigan though. After the disappointment of relegation at Blues, it was just what I needed. They gave me another lease of life and helped me get back into England contention. I had a great relationship with the supporters too. They were easy to please. I went out and enjoyed my football and worked hard and they appreciated it. They weren't the kind of fans to boo their own players. They were loyal and supportive.

I haven't been back in a while to the stadium, but I've visited the training ground since retiring and I can see that they are bringing some good, young players through their academy. Any young player being released from a big club like

United, City or Liverpool in the North West should definitely consider Wigan as a place to go, play and develop.

I can't write about my time at Wigan without mentioning Dave Whelan, the club's influential former chairman. Dave was a great owner and a really nice guy. He gave his all for the club and for the town. I didn't have too many dealings with him but he was very well liked. He understood the game being a former player himself. He backed the players and managers, and was always supportive. Sometimes I feel he was taken advantage of, particularly by the media, who could easily get a quote from him, but I guess he wanted to get messages across. He reflected the way the club was run; it was a great family club, a place where I loved playing and one I'll always look back on with a smile.

CHAPTER ELEVEN

The Gaffer and Wembley? It's History Repeating

I DIDN'T need any persuasion to sign for Aston Villa and the move happened very quickly. Aside from the size of the club and the manager in charge, the challenge of being able to play at the top end of the Premier League again was something I couldn't wait to take on.

Coming from the Midlands, I know what a massive club Villa are but I don't think everyone appreciates just how big. I also looked at their squad when I joined; young, talented players like Gabby Agbonlahor, Ashley Young, James Milner, and then names such as Gareth Barry, John Carew and Stan Petrov. They had talent right the way through the side and with Martin in charge, you knew the squad would be motivated.

I had always loved Villa Park. It was one of my three favourite old-style stadiums to play at. There was something about the place; an aura, the atmosphere and the close proximity of the fans to the pitch is what made it so special. Villa Park, Anfield and White Hart Lane made the hairs stand up on the back of your neck. Filbert Street was special too, but these stadiums were double the size. I was lucky enough to play for two of the clubs who played at those stadiums, and I enjoyed playing at White Hart Lane many times too.

Villa was always going to be tough but having the gaffer there to support me meant a lot. I hadn't played for him for nearly a decade. I'd changed a great deal in that time. I was no longer the young lad leading the line at Leicester, able to take a game by the scruff of the neck and dominate it with pace and power. I was experienced and I'd had to adapt my game many times to suit the system of play and the club. I couldn't affect a game like I had done, despite still being a good player. I was realistic. I'd lost some of my pace and I'd experienced a few injuries. Between the age of 18 and 24 I felt unstoppable, but time catches up on you a little, and I learned to prioritise my positional sense and not just rely upon being quicker than my opponent.

I think that the player I'd become, if I'm honest, probably frustrated both Martin and I. I wanted to burst through defences and brush defenders aside as if they weren't there, but I couldn't do that anymore. I couldn't give Martin what I gave him at Leicester, but I still had a lot to offer. We both got on with it. I would have run through brick walls for that man, so I was determined to repay the faith he showed in me. I didn't want to let him down.

There was plenty of competition to start at Villa with John Carew, Agbonlahor and Marlon Harewood there. I was actually offered Marlon's shirt number when I joined, but I took the number 18 instead. I didn't believe in taking someone else's number; that wasn't the way I did things. Imagine how he would have felt and how I would have been viewed in the dressing room by the other guys. The number I wore didn't really bother me.

* * *

As I had a habit of switching clubs between the Midlands and the North West, I didn't move house on this occasion. I kept my place in the North West and also rented a small place near to Villa and would stay over at times. At a later date, I stayed at a friend's house towards the end of my contract. The commute wasn't too bad. The M6 was busy but I'd get up early and get on the road. In winter it could be bad, especially if it snowed, but it didn't bother me. I drove myself most of the time. Every now and again I would have a driver, but I didn't feel that I needed that. I'd be at Villa's training ground, Bodymoor Heath, in time for breakfast and would train, have lunch and then drive home. I think it's a mental barrier for some players who don't want to drive for that long, but I could be home in just over an hour or so.

I scored on my debut against Portsmouth, having scored against them for Wigan a few weeks before, so Jamo and Sol must have been sick of the sight of me. I flicked the ball on, turned instinctively to see Gabby win the ball and I followed up and scored. I grabbed another goal in April against West Ham and we finished sixth in the Premier League. Martin and the club were trying to push on to break into the Champions League places, but we were a little short where we needed it. You have to spend a fair bit of money to attract the type of players that are required for a top-four finish, and the consistency in your performances has to be there too. Martin did bring some quality footballers into the club, but those he inherited he improved as well. He always had a knack of getting more out of people, and giving them the confidence to believe in themselves and to play for him.

When I look back at Villa at that time, I don't think the ownership was prepared to spend big; I mean really big, to compete with the top clubs. I understand that. You have to either accept that you are outside of the top four and be satisfied, or you need a plan to join them.

Martin always believed he could get Villa to that next level and I think it was difficult for him to take, as he knew we were close. We had Gabby, Milner, Young and Barry, and Petrov, who had won so much with the gaffer at Celtic. Gabby was the local lad who'd come through with expectation on his shoulders, much like I had at Leicester. I got on well with him, and on his day you couldn't stop him. He was quick and powerful, but Gabby probably lacked the consistency to go to the very top of the game.

Was he willing to learn? Yes and no. To reach the top you have to embrace everything, soak it up and be completely dedicated. I didn't feel like Gabby was like that, but he had so much respect for the gaffer that he never once stepped out of line, or spoke badly of Martin. Just as he had at Leicester, Martin had the fear factor around him, but as he treated the players as adults and as long as you gave him everything, he would do anything for you.

Once the lads worked out that if you'd won a game, a big game, and one of you shouted out for days off, he'd just give you them. We'd win on the Saturday and then be off until Thursday. Martin was impulsive like that and would give the lads what they wanted. They loved him for it. Some of the lads would be off for three nights in Dubai and he didn't mind. If you did it for him on the pitch, then you were alright with him. Sometimes, I felt that this meant we weren't quite training as hard as we could have, but I would never question his methods as he got the results and created a strong togetherness wherever he went. He hadn't changed; he was still the same Martin I knew at Leicester. The Villa lads from that era still talk about him now, just like the Leicester lads do, and they all love him and tell stories about him. He's held in such high regard and that takes quite a bit when it comes to footballers.

I settled in well at Villa. They were a friendly bunch and the set-up at the club was great. I'd been through it all before. I was no longer that kid lost in Liverpool, without any idea what to do and where to go, staring up at the ceiling with tears in my eyes. There was a lovely woman called Lorna McClelland who was the club's player liaison officer and she would help to take care of everything for you and your family. She was great with helping to create a family atmosphere, even down to little details like creating a crèche in the players' lounge to allow our families to watch the game, which wasn't something that was common back then. Lorna organised family outings for the group; meals and nights out, which helped to integrate our professional and personal lives, which I know the lads were all very grateful to her for. It felt like a family club. Even now, I'll get WhatsApp messages from the likes of Stan, Fabian Delph, Gabby, Ashley, Marlon, Stephen Ireland, Darren Bent and Nigel Reo-Coker, and we're often talking about getting together for a meal and drinks. That unity has lasted over time and that shows what a special time it was.

In the summer of 2009, Martin strengthened the squad by bringing in Stewart Downing, Fabian, Habib Beye, Stephen Warnock, James Collins and Richard Dunne. Stewy was a great signing, an immense talent; quick, dynamic and would take people on and look to get the ball into the box. As a striker, that's the kind of winger you want supplying service to you. I didn't know much about Fabian, but as soon as he joined it was clear that he loved a tackle and could be a bit of a hot-head at times.

He picked up a bad knee injury early on, so he was unlucky with his time at Villa. I think he found adjusting from Leeds to Birmingham quite tough, like I had with my Leicester to Liverpool move, but Fabian was open about it, which was good, whereas I bottled it up. I think that helped him to get over that feeling. He became a key figure and has gone on to have a fantastic career. James and Richard were solid signings. Martin loved those guys. They would head everything out and tackle relentlessly. He loved their work ethic and the fact that they would even play through injury for the club.

James had a swollen foot after booting someone accidentally. He took his boot off and couldn't get it back on. So, something like a piece of cold steak was laid on his foot to help with the swelling, and then he put a boot on which was a couple of sizes bigger and went out and played. Unbelievable. What a warrior he was. They were old-fashioned centre-backs and strikers knew they'd been in a battle against those two.

Gareth was sold that summer, which was a huge loss for the club. He was relatively quiet, but did all his talking on the pitch. He was a captain who would lead by example. His attitude was spot on, and he was respected by everyone. We relied upon him, so I think he was a big hole to fill for us.

We were knocked out of the Europa League on away goals by Rapid Vienna in the play-off round, which was a big disappointment. We all believed that we could go far in Europe, but I'm not sure whether the club was quite ready for it. As it turned out, we were destined to have two fantastic cup runs that season anyway. In the League Cup, we knocked out

Cardiff City, Sunderland and Portsmouth then Blackburn Rovers over two legs in the semi-final. I scored against Pompey and in the second leg against Blackburn, which we won 6-4, despite being 2-0 down early on. Having won 1-0 away in the first leg, we went through 7-4 on aggregate. I slipped as I scored my goal, and was grateful it went in as I was staring at an empty net.

In the final, we faced Manchester United. That was a huge day for us and for the fans. We went ahead after five minutes when Gabby broke clear and was hauled down by Nemanja Vidic for a penalty, which James Milner scored. Vidic could have easily been sent off for that challenge under the rules at the time. Michael Owen equalised for United and then went off injured and was replaced by Wayne Rooney who got the winner. I had chances that day, and hit the bar late on with a deflected header as we chased the equaliser. The gaffer trusted me to play in a cup final and we were unlucky not to at least take them to extra-time. I would have loved to win that final and to have made it five League Cups wins out of six finals in my career, but it wasn't to be. I would have loved to have won something with Villa. I know we gave the fans some great days out, but to have lifted a trophy at Wembley would have been special.

I can remember Steve Walford telling me to go out and win the final and equal Ian Rush's record of five wins, but we fell just short. The Villa fans loved that season though; reaching a final at Wembley, and there was never any talk of playing a weakened team like Premier League sides do now. The gaffer just wouldn't have considered that at all.

We reached the semi-finals of the FA Cup, losing 3-0 to Chelsea, but it was another Wembley appearance and we felt as if we were getting closer to success, moving in the right direction. Martin was driving us on and we were just fine margins away from reaching the top table.

I scored five goals that season in 26 starts and 16 substitute appearances. We finished sixth, as we did the season before, qualifying for the Europa League play-off round again. We just didn't have enough to take that next step. I think there's only so much you can do and I guess that the owner at the time, Randy Lerner, would say that there wasn't any further funds he could have thrown at it. We'll never know how far we could have gone, but I'm sure that we would have continued to progress and achieved success under Martin if he'd have been backed again. The best clubs would continue to invest year-on-year and if you don't, then you fall further behind them.

As best as I can remember, no one saw what was to come in the next pre-season. Martin resigned just a few days before the start of the season. It came totally out of the blue. I didn't have a clue it was going to happen. I couldn't believe it. We were five days from the first game. I'm not sure where Martin was mentally at that point, with regard to looking at his squad and feeling, 'Have I taken this group as far as I can?' Given that we only made one signing that summer, Stephen Ireland, which was part of the deal that saw James Milner go

Jumping for joy! The winning goal in the last minute of the final game of the season, to beat Arsenal. I was proud to finish as top scorer and players' and supporters' player of the season at Blues.

Nerves of steel. David Unsworth, who had signed for Wigan Athletic from Sheffield United, scored the penalty which relegated his former club, and kept us in the top flight. I finished this game as a centre-back heading balls out of the box, using my skills from the young vs old training games at Leicester to keep us safe.

Antoine Sibierski loved the English game, but couldn't believe how much we tackled and that losing sides would never give up. He was technically one of the best players I played with.

I didn't believe it was Steve McClaren on the end of the phone, telling me I was back in the England squad. Football dressing rooms are full of pranksters, but this was real. Michael Owen was instrumental in getting me back in the fold as he told Steve that he wanted me to partner him up front.

A new sheriff in town. Fabio Capello was strict, but I found him fine to work with. He picked me in his first squad and I played for him through to the 2010 World Cup.

Joining the 100 club. My goal for Wigan Athletic at Portsmouth in November 2008 gave us all three points, but it was also my 100th Premier League goal. To be part of that club of strikers is something I'll always be proud of.

A debut goal. Just a few weeks after doing it for Wigan, I was back at Fratton Park scoring, this time for my new club, Aston Villa. I was so pleased to be playing for Martin O'Neill again, and for such a big club.

This is the last time. My last goal in an England shirt came against Kazakhstan away from home. It was a tap in, nothing special, but it was my seventh goal for my country at senior level. I know people think I should have got more, maybe they are right, but I was proud to get as many as I did.

Ten-goal thriller at the Villa. Here I am scoring the fifth goal for Villa in a 6-4 win over Blackburn Rovers in the 2010 League Cup semi-final second leg. I rounded Paul Robinson, slipped, scored and the gaffer and I were heading back to Wembley.

Captain Fantastic. What a player Steven Gerrard was for Liverpool and England. Here he is leading from the front and scoring in our opening 2010 World Cup game against the USA. Stevie was one of the best players I played with and it's no surprise he's gone in to management. He's a born leader.

They think it's all over...and for me it was. My last time in an England shirt was quite fittingly against Germany, but sadly it came in a 4-1 defeat as we exited the 2010 World Cup. I pulled the famous jersey on 62 times and I wouldn't swap that experience for the world. Not bad for a boy from Highfields.

Not for the first time. Back with Gerard Houllier, but this time at Aston Villa. I felt sad that things didn't work out for Gerard in the Midlands. That dressing room just wanted to play for Martin, and anyone who had walked in after him was up against it.

Boiling point. Referee Mike Jones shows me the yellow card, but all I could see was the red mist after being persistently elbowed and struck by Antolin Alcaraz. I took myself off at half-time to prevent anything worse happening.

The Marquee Men. From left to right: Shinji Ojo of Western Sydney Wanderers, me representing Newcastle Jets and Alessandro Del Piero of Sydney FC, at a photoshoot for the start of the 2012/13 season.

You've still got it, kid. My first goal for Newcastle Jets, against Sydney FC. I loved my time in Australia. The culture, the people, the lifestyle was incredible and the football was really enjoyable too. When I left, I was ready to come home to be with my family, and for one last taste of English football.

You'll never walk alone. Returning to Anfield with my final club, Bolton Wanderers, for an FA Cup fourth round tie in January 2015 was emotional. Receiving a standing ovation from the crowd left me speechless.

Hello, old friend. Neil Lennon gave me another chance to play in England, with Bolton Wanderers, which I'll always be grateful for. I lost count of how many times I called him Lenny, instead of gaffer in front of the rest of the squad.

Old School. I may have retired from playing, but I took great pride from working with Leicester after their incredible Premier League title win, here, on their US tour, sharing a joke with Hollywood star, Will Ferrell.

My beautiful, talented wife Chantelle, and wonderful mother to four of my children. We fell in love and we are a partnership. Chan is my best friend, she understands me and I'll always be there for her.

Since retiring, I've done a lot of media work and charitable appearances, as well as ambassadorial work for my former clubs. I still want to be involved directly in the game though. It's in my blood. I'd love to coach and mentor younger players in an academy. I feel like I've still got a lot to give.

to Manchester City, the writing was on the wall in terms of spending, or a lack of it. He walked away and that was the end of an era. Martin was fiercely ambitious and he would not have tolerated the club dropping down the league and not competing in the cups.

He passionately wanted to bring trophies to Villa Park. I know he's had some stick from fans for leaving that close to the start of the season, but I respect his reasons for doing it. The job and the club were changing and it wasn't the role that was sold to him when he joined. As players, we didn't have time to dwell on it as Kevin MacDonald took over temporary charge of the side, and we had to be prepared. We were again knocked out in the play-off round of the Europa League, and once more it was Rapid Vienna. I scored in the second leg, a 3-2 home defeat, and we lost 4-3 on aggregate. It wasn't a great start to the season. Rapid just had our number, like some teams do.

Losing Milner was huge, in a similar way to losing Barry the year before. James was a mainstay, a hugely important player within our team. If you are going to kick on, as Martin wanted, and win cups or challenge the top four, you can't afford to lose players like him. You can't begrudge someone wanting to move on, to try to fulfil their own ambitions, but as a player who stays behind after their departure, you begin to question the ambition of the club, which is obviously what must have been Martin's thought process as well. I didn't have much contact with Randy. He was a nice man, and I felt for him as you can't just keep spending. He obviously had deep pockets but wasn't prepared to keep dipping into them as some investors do. It's his money and therefore his call, but I can see why the fans became frustrated.

* * *

There were other great players at the club, so it wasn't a mass exodus yet. Ashley was pure class, a game-changer for us. He had a knack of going down the left wing, chopping the ball back and curling it into dangerous areas. What has impressed me hugely is the way that he has adapted his career over time, playing at left-back for Manchester United and England. He has a superb football brain, he was a hard worker and a bubbly person, always full of fun. In fact, training at Villa was great fun, which was because of the strong characters we had at the time. Ashley was the kind who would roll his ankle in a game, and by Thursday he would be back training and would play on the Saturday as if nothing had happened. He always cared.

John Carew, well, what can I say? I hope he doesn't mind me saying this, as I mean it with all due respect and a bit tongue-in-cheek, but I think football interfered with John's social life. That's probably the easiest way of saying it. He wasn't actually that far off being as quick as Gabby, but double his size, so who was going to stop him? He was a machine. John had a great career. He could score goals, could hold the ball up and he was a star player. He wanted to live his life, and the daily life of being a prepared, professional footballer just didn't quite fit with him. I wasn't at the club for some of the alleged stories, but he was a funny guy; I'll leave it at that.

After Kevin's month in the hot seat, it was time to be reunited with yet another former manager of mine, Gerard Houllier, and his assistant Gary McAllister. It was great for me. I knew them well and respected them both. It was always going to be difficult to replace Martin, as he'd built something really special within the squad at Villa. Whoever followed was going to be directly compared to Martin and was going to bring their own players in, which would change the feeling in the dressing room. Gerard was very different to Martin as well. They were polar opposites. Things were a lot more structured and stringent under Gerard and the lads probably didn't take to that very well. When it came to training methods, I think they struggled to adapt to his ways. I was used to his ways, but he never came to me to ask for my help with communicating his message. I could have helped as a senior player, but he had Macca who could do that for him.

It's easy to look back in hindsight, but I think the odds were stacked against Gerard. He didn't have the summer to get the players to understand his football philosophy, and also missed the first month of the season, so that was tough. I can remember feeling like I was going to fall asleep when I joined Liverpool as I sat in on meetings; I wasn't used to the level of detail that was required. That was brought in at Villa and was a bit of a culture shock for the lads as well. You're in a dark room, with the screen on and you can feel your eyes getting heavy. At Leicester it was very brief under Martin and I liked that, as I only really focused on myself at that age, but as you get older you realise the responsibility that you have to take on as a senior player, and you should know about your opponent. You don't want to have to figure out your opponent when you're already on the pitch and facing him.

I scored a couple of goals in the League Cup in wins over Blackburn Rovers and Burnley, before we were knocked out by our rivals Birmingham City in the quarter-finals. I was lucky that I never once felt any negativity from either Villa or Blues about playing for the other one. I guess the fact that I signed for Wigan in between helped as I wasn't making the direct move. I was probably seen more as a Leicester or Liverpool player so I escaped any of the stick. I still see fans of both Villa and Blues now, and they'll argue over which side I preferred playing for, which is nice.

In the January, Gerard brought Darren Bent in from Sunderland and while it seemed as if the club's investment was starting to decrease, Darren was a club record signing, so there was still some backing there at least, although I think this signing was a necessity to ensure we didn't get dragged into a relegation dogfight.

The season took a shocking turn in April though, when Gerard suffered chest pains, at first thought to be a heart attack, which was later ruled out. Gerard had to rest, while Macca took over until the end of the season.

It was very difficult for him to step into the role, just as Phil Thompson had done for Gerard at Liverpool years earlier. We had a strong dressing room at Villa; they were vocal, lots of leaders, and I felt that Macca, or whoever was going to step in, would have struggled with that. There was only one man who could have coped with it all, and that was Martin.

The gaffer would just walk in and silence them all. He had such a commanding presence.

People would be standing up, shouting, arguing and when he walked in and told people to be quiet, they were quiet and sat down within seconds. It was also tough for Macca as he was seen as a coach, or number two, and it's always difficult to switch from that role, where you are seen as a friend to the players, to being the gaffer. That's not his fault, that's just how football is structured.

In May, I was involved in an incident in our home game against my former club, Wigan. I was elbowed by Antolin Alcaraz and was justifiably fuming about it. I believe it was deliberate and no one will convince me otherwise. I wasn't being protected by the officials as it wasn't a one-off either. Players can go up to challenge for the ball with their elbows out to the side, but he led with his elbow in front of him, hitting me in the back of the head on more than one occasion. I've come off the pitch with lumps on my head before, but known that was part of the game. This was different. I was being targeted. I lost it. I completely saw red.

I barged into the referee Mike Jones as I felt like he should have been doing more, and I actually took myself off at half-time. It was reported that I was substituted, but that wasn't the case. I spoke to Macca and told him that I couldn't go back out there as I'd either end up badly injured or sent off. If I'd have gone back on for the second half, there would have been trouble one way or another. I know myself. I had to be restrained at one point. It was tough, with around four or five people holding on to me. I wanted to get to Alcaraz, in the tunnel – yes, me, tunnels and fighting again – but I was stopped. Everyone has their triggers and their limits, and I had gone way past mine. I want to be clear here; this wasn't one stray elbow, it was persistent and targeted. I'm normally a pretty calm and relaxed guy, but I would bet that most people would have reacted the way I did that day. It left a nasty taste in the mouth, something that I haven't forgotten to this day.

I scored six goals in the 2010/11 season, and we'd had a poor year, but somehow managed to drag ourselves up to finish in ninth place. There were the off-field difficulties with manager changes and Gerard's health issues, and on the field we were nowhere near the standards we'd set. We were struggling towards the bottom, and won our last two games, away to Arsenal and at home to Liverpool. The club was in a transitional period and I think we lacked a bit of identity and certainly consistency.

After the season finished, Gerard left the club because of his health situation. I don't think he was left with any other choice. It was very sad for him. If you have that number of scares then you need to put yourself first. He was always putting others first and had that fatherly nature about him. I don't think that Villa saw the best of him, to be honest, not like we did at Liverpool. As I've said, it's such a stressful job being a manager, so I know he did the right thing for him and his family.

He was replaced by Alex McLeish, in quite controversial circumstances given that he'd just been relegated, but more importantly, he was moving to us directly from Birmingham City. To give context, he'd also just won the League Cup with them, beating Arsenal in the final. He'd had a successful time as a manager at Rangers and came with a reputation. The move directly across the city was pretty intense though. As I've said, I had my time at Wigan to break it up. I saw Nick Barmby and Abel Xavier do the move across Liverpool, and that was tough for them both too. McLeish was off to a negative start, with some fans even demonstrating against the appointment. I know it's only football, but it's people's lives and sometimes you have to listen to your supporters and what they want for their club. If you look at it, a former Blues boss who had just been relegated was not going to get everyone excited. I felt like he was walking into a difficult situation, similar to what Gerard had come in to after Martin left, but this was worse than that. There were still strong characters around, who were perhaps stuck in their ways, and it needed an equally tough character to turn the tide.

I didn't feel like I had a great deal of communication with Alex. I wasn't playing that well under him in all fairness, and spent a lot of time on the bench, coming on as a left winger, late on in games, more like a bit-part player. I was into my final year with the club, so I could see what was coming.

In the summer, Leicester City came in for me, as Sven-Göran Eriksson was their manager and he was bringing some decent names to the club as they geared up to try to win promotion back to the Premier League. I went to see Alex to discuss the situation, but he just said that Villa needed me. I would have loved to go back to play for Leicester again. I didn't mind dropping down a division either.

McLeish blocked the move, but I felt like there were young players who could have done my role for Villa. If I was starting games regularly, then maybe I could have understood it. Leicester would have to pay a fee and I was coming towards the end of my contract anyway, but it wasn't to be. I didn't kick off about the situation. I wasn't the kind of player to try to force a move or refuse to play. I didn't have time for players who did that. I just got my head down and played for Villa, but inside I was disappointed to have not been given the chance for an emotional return to my hometown club.

I think Leicester had a three-year deal on the table for me and, regardless of how much I'd changed as a player, I would have given everything for the club. I thought McLeish would have understood that and let me go. He'd been a player himself and he knew how much Leicester meant to me. I was under contract though, and that was the end of it. I would have finished my career at Leicester, which would have been nice. I don't hate McLeish but I do blame him for denying me that opportunity.

* * *

McLeish brought Shay Given, Alan Hutton and Charles N'Zogbia in during the summer, but we lost a number of players. Robert Pires was one; even though he was older by the time he played for Villa, he still had a great impact on games. Bobby still had so much ability but maybe not the legs to play in that Villa side for the style of play. Nigel left too and he was a real leader around the dressing room and was a solid player. He was one of the key players for us for years, and along with others like Brad Friedel, Ashley, Stewart, John and Luke Young, there was an exodus of that core of the squad.

Brad was a fantastic goalkeeper. He was a superb professional and always had a positive influence on young players. Ashley was wonderful for Villa, and I think Charles coming in was as a direct replacement and that was a lot of expectation placed on his shoulders. I could see the shift in the squad; we were losing our best players and that means you only go one way and that's down the league table. We were still working hard, but we didn't have the quality to rely upon anymore.

McLeish wasn't an old-fashioned manager as such. He tried to be open-minded and embrace modern methods, but it just didn't work for him. The players didn't seem to embrace him, like they didn't Gerard during his time at the club. It felt as if the shadow of Martin O'Neill was cast over everyone still. We finished 16th and escaped relegation by just two points, which was unthinkable at the time. Since then, Villa have experienced relegation, but at the time, that season was seen as a disaster and the manager paid the price with his job. It was a gradual deterioration during my time at Villa once Martin had left. We didn't win any of our final ten league games under McLeish, so it was no wonder that he left at the end of the season.

The sadness at the club had started a couple of months earlier with something so much more important than football. Stan Petrov was our skipper, our man, our legend. He was loved by everyone at the club and he typified what we were about as a club during those years. The fans adored him.

We played Arsenal away in March and a player ran off the back of Stan, he didn't track him and they scored. That was out of character for him and he didn't quite look himself. He was still running around and trying, but he wasn't as effective or as sharp as normal. Stan wasn't feeling well and, remember, this was just a week after Fabrice Muamba had suffered a heart attack at the Spurs versus Bolton game.

Stan said he'd not felt himself for the week leading up to the game, and that his legs weren't right during the game. We lost 3-0 so it was a bad day and the manager was angry with the way we'd performed. Stan had wanted to come off at half-time, but the lads persuaded him to stay on as we needed him. He went home afterwards and still felt ill, with no energy.

After what had happened with Fabrice, it was compulsory to do heart checks and the club doctor did that, with us running on the treadmill, and then he took blood samples as well. Within a couple of days, Stan was diagnosed with acute leukaemia. It was essential for him to be treated as soon as possible. I was so naive. I comforted Stan as we all did and then I asked him when we'd see him playing again. I couldn't imagine him not playing for us. This was our captain. He said he probably wouldn't be playing again. I didn't mean to be insensitive, but as footballers we always talk in those terms. We all want to be out there playing. In 2013 he retired from the game, but a few years later he returned to training with Villa and was available to play in pre-season, which was an incredible achievement after all he had been through.

After the season finished and McLeish left, I already knew that my future didn't lie at Villa; there was never a conversation about extending my deal. People knew that the writing was on the wall for McLeish and that's why the Leicester deal not happening frustrated me so much. There was no manager at the club when I left, as Paul Lambert was appointed a few weeks after my departure. Brad Guzan was in the same situation, but then he was brought back by Paul. Brad did very well for the club, but often Shay Given would play instead, and he was an excellent goalkeeper. I was ready to leave though. I'd enjoyed three and a half years at Villa but

I think I'd gone a bit stale by then, just as the team had, and there wasn't a future at the club for me anyway.

There were so many names at Villa who I played with, and hopefully I won't have forgotten anyone in this chapter. Steve Sidwell was a quality midfielder, but he had such a lot of competition to fight against. Darren Bent was a superb goalscorer, but we needed someone he could play off. He had to spend a lot of time with his back to goal in our system and that didn't suit his style, as he was a poacher who wanted the ball in behind.

Marc Albrighton was young at the time and he was one of the best crossers of a ball I have ever played with. When he left Villa, he asked me about joining Leicester and I said he would love it there and they would love him. I don't think anyone would have expected him to have the level of success he's had, but he deserves everything as he's such a good character and is as hard-working as they come. I couldn't understand why Villa were letting him go at the time, and that decision looks even worse now. He puts the ball into dangerous areas, exactly where strikers want it, and he loved the club. That was a strange one, but worked out well for him.

Another young lad I remember well was Ciaran Clark and, indirectly, I gave him his debut. Martin had seen me play at centre-back for Wigan in the infamous relegation decider against Sheffield United and asked me to play there for Villa one game. I politely refused. I say politely, but I think I laughed at Martin and made it clear there was no way I could do it. That Wigan game was just a few minutes, but 90 minutes at the back wouldn't have been great for me, or for Villa. Martin wasn't happy with me, but I would have been out of position, whereas the Sheffield United game was just heading and booting the ball out as we were camped in our own penalty area. Ciaran was then given his first start and never looked back.

I have nothing but good things to say about my time at Villa and about the fans. They just want, and deserve, good football and success. We gave them a taste of it under Martin, but couldn't quite win a trophy and then we started to slide when he left. The Villa fans want players who will fight and will give their all, no different to other fans. They have pride, and for a long time, especially when I was younger, they were the biggest club in the Midlands. I loved my time at the club. I will look back with some disappointment that our side was broken up and replaced with players who weren't as good, and it's a shame that we weren't able to carry on as we did during my year and a half under Martin.

As I've said though, the writing was on the wall and everyone could see it happening. We lost Gareth, James, Ashley and many more, and it's hard enough replacing one of them, let alone all of them. I don't think we were run properly during my final two seasons at the club either. I'm not pointing fingers at anyone, but the evidence is there. If Martin had stayed and been given support, that side would have gone on to bigger and better things, I'm sure of it.

CHAPTER TWELVE

Down Under ... the Wanderer Returns

I LEFT Villa without knowing where I was going and what was next for me. It was the first time in my career that had happened. I thought I'd have no problems finding a club as that was how it had always been. Time ticked by and I trained with the Wigan under-21s for a month or so and I waited by my phone but nothing came.

I kept myself busy with media work and legends football, and then my agent suggested I join Blackpool, as lots of players were signing for them, but they were a club in trouble at the time and I didn't fancy that. Once you are through the summer, it can be difficult to get in at a club as managers want players who are match fit and can hit the ground running. I knew I was towards the end of my playing days but I still felt I could offer a club something. I had no intentions of retiring yet.

Out of the blue, Robbie Fowler called me. He had played for Queensland Fury and Perth Glory and asked if I'd be interested in playing in Australia. I asked him about the standard and the way of life and he sold it to me. The guy he'd played with was the chief executive officer at Newcastle Jets, Robbie Middleby, and the club sent an offer over to me, and I accepted. It all happened pretty quickly. If I'd have had an offer to stay in England, I probably would have, denying me the experience of playing on the other side of the world. I'm glad I took that path.

I didn't go over for a trial or look at the club and the area. I just signed, as they wanted me to decide quickly. That was pretty impulsive for me, but all my moves in my career seemed to happen without any fuss. I took the long flight to the other side of the world and began my new life in Australia.

There was a huge media presence at the airport and I had a press conference to get through as soon as I landed. I wasn't expecting all the fanfare but they made a big deal out of my arrival, which was nice of them. I would have preferred to have just got in the car and unpacked at my apartment, but that's not the style with football clubs. I had a training session on that first day and then I just slept and slept. I would get up for some food and drink every few hours and then go back to bed. I've never experienced jet lag like that.

I was classed as the club's marquee signing, and along with Alessandro Del Piero and Shinji Ono, I was one of the A-League's marquee players too. I initially moved out there on my own, as the kids were young and had just started school. They had made friends already and it made sense not to disrupt their lives as well. The football season only lasted six months, so I was able to have them over with my wife at Christmas and New Year, and I would be back home in England as soon as the season was over.

I lived in Newcastle itself. It's a mining town, a decent size, on the coast and the weather was great. The people were working class and down to earth and I enjoyed every minute of my time there. The town centre was quite small, and I found the place quite quiet which suited me at that stage in my life. I was in an apartment overlooking the beach and the sea. It was beautiful. I was looked after very well. I didn't venture into the water, I have to say, as I didn't trust what was in there – sharks. It's an incredible place for surfers though and I'd often sit on my balcony and see dolphins leaping while people were surfing. I'd swim in the sea water in rock pools nearby, knowing I was safe, and we'd often use these pools as warm-downs after training. It was a great way of life.

The facilities at the club weren't the best. We trained at the university, which was a pitch and a pavilion and nothing much else. It did what it needed to do. I would take my own kit and boots home with me and wash them. It was like going back to the start of my career at Leicester and I didn't mind that at all. We would eat at the university after training and you'd have to buy your own lunch, which was something I hadn't ever done as a footballer, but again, it was a humbling experience, which was good for me.

The stadium was really nice, and we shared that with the rugby club, so the pitch would take a bit of a hammering. Football is behind rugby league and cricket in Australia, particularly rugby league in Newcastle, as the Knights had won a couple of titles and were very proud of that. I was recognised, but not mobbed, and that relative anonymity was a nice change of pace compared to life in England.

I enjoyed going out and eating in the town centre. I think it was King Street, where they had a lot of independent coffee shops, and lots of places serving locally sourced fruit and vegetables. I was eating really healthily and found the way of life so appealing. It's easy to look out of the window here in Cheshire some days, even though it's a beautiful area of the country, and look at the grey clouds, the wind and the rain and think about life on the other side of the world. That's the thing though, it's the other side of the world, and I would struggle to be that far away from England and my friends and family. It's an amazing place though. People smile and seem so happy and that's a lot to do with the weather and having a more outdoors lifestyle. When my kids visited, we went to a park and they were playing with other kids and climbing trees. I'd never seen them climb a tree before. The sunshine really does bring the best out of people.

The club operated with a European coaching set-up, with Gary van Egmond in the head coach role, and a heavy

Dutch influence on the coaching style. He was a very good and knowledgeable coach, who I could see would be effective coaching younger players, working on specific technical improvements in their game. I understood what he was trying to do, but some of the players didn't engage as well as they could have, as he gave a lot of information and detail.

To offer a comparison to England, I felt that the standard of football was probably similar to the Championship for the better clubs and maybe League One for those lower down the A-League. We played out from the back on every occasion, with the goalkeeper not allowed to kick the ball long. Our centre-backs would spread wide to receive the ball, the full-backs would push on and midfielders would drop deep. This was all well and good in theory, but we simply didn't have the standard of players to play this way and as soon as they were put under pressure we would panic and either give the ball away, or boot it clear. You have to have defenders who are comfortable with the ball at their feet, and a team who will constantly move, creating angles and space to receive the ball. You always need trust, and if you see a team-mate give the ball away once, you'll think twice about giving it back to them. Brisbane were probably the only side who had the personnel to play like that, but it was good to see that we were at least trying to develop this ethos and philosophy.

I enjoyed the responsibility of being a senior player, and helping the younger lads, who clearly wanted to learn and develop. I was working just as hard as everyone else, as I wanted to show my standards hadn't dropped towards the end of my career. I scored nine goals in 23 matches and was nominated for the player of the season award.

I had a knack of doing really well in my first full season with a club. It happened at Leicester, Liverpool, Birmingham, Wigan and Villa, and I repeated it for Newcastle Jets. I loved the whole experience and felt like I was still learning even though I was older now. I had always wanted to get out of England and try playing abroad. When I was younger, I would look at the likes of David Platt, Paul Ince and Gazza playing in Italy and while this was not the same, it was still an experience away from England. Everyone rams the Premier League down your throat as a player and the hype that comes with it means that not many English players end up going abroad. That's a shame. I would urge young players to go abroad and experience it. My only regret, if I have one, is that I didn't go abroad earlier in my career, but I'm grateful I had the opportunity anyway. I wanted to get out of the bubble and to not have the need to 'keep up with the Joneses' all the time in England.

I signed a new contract for the 2013/14 season and played 19 times that campaign. It wasn't the best year for me as I injured my medial ligaments in pre-season, which was probably one of the biggest injuries of my career. I struggled as a result and anyone who has been through that will tell you that their knee feels floppy. It's a weird sensation and a strange injury. You don't feel like you can control your own knee. I found turning, running, passing a ball, all basic things within the game, very difficult all of a sudden and you need time to recover.

I was contemplating staying on for another year, but I was missing my family and I felt like I'd scratched that itch of living and playing abroad and I needed to come home. I still follow Newcastle Jets from afar now. The people were so kind to me and the fans were great. The club has had some financial issues over the years and to run a club like that, you need a fair bit of money to maintain the standards as I don't think they get a huge amount of revenue from the league itself. I hope they can continue to progress in the future, as I'll always be a fan. When I think back, I picture my debut, against Sydney FC, who had Del Piero, and there were 45,000 people packed into the stadium. It was something else and showed the potential for football out there. Australian people have a huge passion for sport, but there are so many other sports to choose from, so football often misses out. There's a large population of Europeans, particularly from Eastern Europe in Australia, and that passion for football within the country will continue to grow, I'm sure of it.

I returned home to the UK and knew I wanted to play again. I trained with Blackburn Rovers, with their manager Gary Bowyer kindly allowing me to work with them to keep me ticking over, but I was still hoping for something more permanent. One last crack at it. My old Leicester team-mate Neil Lennon was the manager at Bolton Wanderers, and his assistant was Garry Parker, whose boots I'd cleaned all those years ago. Parks said I could come to train with them. Bolton were struggling for money, so a free transfer would appeal to them.

They threw me into an under-21s game and while I wasn't really at my best, they'd seen enough to know that I could offer them something. I signed very quickly for Bolton, as a back-up striker. I'd kept in touch with Parks; I've always had a lot of time for him. He's a funny guy and a good bloke. Here I was, again playing for someone I used to work for. It's a lesson to never burn your bridges. We all need a little bit of help from time to time and there's no shame in that. I still had something left to offer. I wasn't as quick, but I could still jump, I was strong and I could play. I had the bit of nous which comes with age in football too. It was great to be back.

I made an early error at Bolton. In front of all the lads I greeted the manager with the words, 'Alright, Lenny?' on my first morning. Neil was good about it and joked, 'I'm fining you if you call me that again, Emile.' No one minded, but it took me a long time to get used to calling him gaffer. He was Lenny, my old team-mate, and Parks too. I wasn't being disrespectful. I just saw them as team-mates and friends. That had to change.

I immediately saw traits of *the* gaffer, Martin O'Neill, in my new gaffer as well. If you've played for someone that influential, you're going to take the best bits from them and use what you can, in the same way that I'm sure Brian

Clough had a strong influence over Martin himself. Lenny was an exceptional footballer, and he's proven himself to be a successful manager too; winning trophies at Celtic, working effectively in a difficult role at Bolton and, more recently, having some success with Hibernian.

At Bolton, he was told he could go and sign a player, and he'd spend the time negotiating with them, get an agreement, and then be told by the club that they didn't have the money, or that he couldn't sign the player. It was a waste of everyone's time and didn't exactly paint Bolton in the best light either. That can put other players off speaking with you as well, as football is a small industry in terms of word of mouth. Lenny did very well in that first season, working with the resources he had. It was a very difficult time for the club and he was the strong leader that we needed.

I made my debut on Boxing Day 2014, scoring an equaliser against Blackburn in a 2-1 win. Afterwards, some of their players came over to me and said they knew that I would score, given that I had been training with them. Football has a funny way of throwing up those kinds of things. I was privileged at Bolton to play alongside Eidur Gudjohnsen. The media picked up on our age and lots of jokes were made about us being an old-age pensioner strikeforce as we were both in our mid-thirties, but we both just wanted to play and loved having the opportunity.

We did well in training as well; we weren't lagging at the back on any tests, we were both near the top or in the middle as we'd looked after ourselves. He was great to play with. Eidur was a very intelligent footballer, always three steps ahead of his opponent, without having to move too much. He would have the ability to create space and time for himself, something that only top players can do. He was effortlessly good. There was also a talented young player there with us at the time, Zach Clough. Bolton should have built everything around him, but he was sold to Nottingham Forest, then came back on loan and wasn't played. He's still young now at the time of writing this, so has time to achieve more and realise that potential. He has very good technical skills, without having blistering pace, but I'm not sure that Bolton played him in his correct position, and obviously given the club's financial issues, he was seen as an asset worth selling to generate funds. Lenny got plenty out of Zach, but it must have been frustrating that he would have to shop in the bargain basement to replace key players.

Bolton is a great club and I played for them in a difficult period in their history. I enjoyed my time there, and was proud to have played for the club. The players were a great bunch too. One difference I did notice though, was that the younger lads coming through didn't take well to criticism. When we were their age, we just had to take the hairdryer treatment and show that we had thick skin. If you reacted back then, you would be shouted at even louder until you accepted the situation. It was always called character-building and for some players it was tough to take.

The lads coming through now won't take being shouted at and are a lot more sensitive. Lenny came through the older era which I experienced, and now you have to be softer, to skirt around the truth with kids to help get the best out of them. I think a lot of managers have had to adapt to this now as well. The fans at Bolton always turned up and backed us, which was tough to do given the issues and the results around the time, so I couldn't fault them. But there was a cloud hanging over the place. At some stage, their club was run into the ground and they suffered for those mistakes. I really felt for them.

It was the right time for me to finish playing after Bolton. My contract had come to an end and I'd made my mind up that I'd had enough. I'd done everything I wanted to do and it was time to move on. There was no chat with Bolton about carrying on and I didn't consider dropping down the leagues either. Once I'd finished, I started to train with Cheshire League club Egerton during pre-season, which was because I was so used to training. I needed the routine and wanted to keep fit and healthy.

There were some other ex-players there like the late Jlloyd Samuel, Dean Gorre, Nathan Ellington, and Emmerson Boyce came down and trained for a bit too. If there were enough of us we would play 11-a-side, but five or seven-a-side was the norm. Robbie Savage coached one of the kids' teams there too. The club is based over in Knutsford, and it was an outlet for me, otherwise I would have been sitting at home,

tearing my hair out. I didn't want to play for them, I just
wanted to train. There's only so much you can do in a gym
without being bored. I enjoyed the camaraderie and it helped
me to get over knowing that I wouldn't play professionally
again. I just enjoyed playing football, like I had all those years
ago as a kid, without a worry in the world.

I don't miss playing now. I miss being around the training
ground, even pre-season. I loved the routine, being with the
lads and it all gave me a purpose. When footballers finish
playing that is all taken away from you. Unless you go into
coaching or management, you can be left without knowing
what to do. It's a scary time and it's no surprise that some lose
their money, or find themselves in a bad way in terms of their
mental or physical health. I don't think footballers will ever
get over finishing being a player. Nothing compares to it. I've
kept myself involved in the game through media work, which I
enjoy. I like watching games and giving a bit of my experience
back. I know you need to go out and get your badges and
qualifications, but I think it's a little sad that former players
like me can have all of that experience, 22 years in the game
in my case, to be told we have no experience to step into the
coaching world.

I could spend time going through my qualifications, but if
I don't get a job then it will have been a waste of time. There
are countless examples of former players out there who are
over-qualified and without a coaching role. I know the game.
I've played for some incredible managers, alongside world-

class players, and I've experienced everything football has to throw at you. I could pass that on. I want to pass that on. I believe I have something to offer. I feel like I've done my work experience, my apprenticeship in the game, and learned on the job, so to speak. There should be a balance there and an appreciation of a playing career being relevant when it comes to coaching. I've completed my Level Two, and the next step would be to get my B licence and A licence, but I'll do that when I'm in a job. I don't want to be a highly educated football coach, just sat on my couch. What's the point in that?

I'd like to help mentor some kids at a club, as well as coach them. I feel like I could give my experience to them. I could help players to prepare for games and help them to learn how to deal with off-field distractions as well. I've witnessed young lads, 16 or 17 years old, struggling to come to terms with their role within football. At that age, I was already in the first team at Leicester gaining first-hand experience. I would encourage lads to go out and gain experience on loan. I was shy, as I've said, but I came to life on the pitch. I could help to get these lads to express themselves and to take their chance when it comes along, before it passes them by.

Bolton gave me an opportunity through Iain Brunskill, who is a very accomplished coach. He was let go, unfortunately, but working alongside him helped me to understand how he did things. I loved it, working with the Bolton under-23s. I would like to get involved at a club again, but often in football it's more a case of who you know, not what you know. I've applied to clubs in the past and haven't even had a reply. I'm not expecting to get every job, but not replying or not even considering me is just disrespectful. My dream role would be to work with Leicester City again; to go full circle and help the kids come through there, where I came through.

I honestly feel as if I have a lot to give back to the game. I would love to be a coach in the future and also believe I could work higher up, maybe as a sporting director, or something like that. I've dealt with players, managers, agents, the media and I know how a football club should work on the playing side. I've worked a little bit with Liverpool and Leicester City with media work and appearances, and I enjoy that a lot, but it's not the same as the coaching side. I want to do a lot more. My heart keeps bringing me back to football. Hopefully I'll get the right opportunity to show what I can do.

CHAPTER THIRTEEN

Meet the Heskeys

I'M a strange person. Seriously, I am. I just like my own time and space. People always want me to go to see this person or to go out somewhere. I'm just happy at home, in my own company or with my family. My wife, Chantelle, will urge me to go out somewhere, and sometimes I just want to be left alone. I like my life the way it is. When you buy a house, you think it's your own castle and you want to be there and enjoy it. It's probably not a good thing as it can make you anti-social, which I don't think I am. I just like being in my own company.

I get asked out for a coffee for meetings or by friends and I just say, 'Yeah, okay, we'll do that soon' but then I don't get round to it. I'll get invited to go to watch Premier League games in an executive box, something most football fans would love to do, and I'll just pass on it. It must be my shyness.

The strange thing about me though, the bit that probably confuses people, is that when you actually get me along to these events, I love it. I suddenly love being around people. I fucking love chatting away with people, being at the centre of it all. It could be social anxiety or nerves, and not wanting to put myself out there. I can be nervous being around people sometimes, but once I'm settled, I love it.

I've spoken about my shyness as a kid, never wanting to leave my mum's side. I knew my dad hated it. He's open and will get involved in anything. I would hold back and I think he thought I was a weird kid, but I was just different to him, that's all. Once I played games or sports, I was fine; table football, pool, cricket, football, you name it and I was good at it and enjoyed it.

Nowadays, I have a busy life. With seven kids, you are always going to be busy. In the evenings, Chantelle would normally cook for us, but now she is very busy with the restaurant she is running, so I'll cook sometimes, or my mother-in-law will. It's difficult to time everything as the kids are playing football in the evenings and we're all on different time schedules.

On a Tuesday and Thursday, I'll pick the kids up from school, get them changed and get some food down them. Then with one on the way to his football, we'll pick another up from nursery and you don't know what state they will be in, having rolled around all day, so they may need to change. I'll be at football from 5pm until around 8pm and then back home, more food and then everyone will be washed, changed and ready for bed. They have busier social lives than I do! I'm there at the school discos, sat at the side waiting for them. It's funny to watch, just like a nightclub used to be for us. We'd buy a load of alcohol and act silly; they buy a load of sweets and fizzy drinks, get high on sugar, dance and run around doing the same. My life with my kids is a full-time job, as there's the morning routine as well, but I wouldn't swap it for the world.

I used to love watching *Def Comedy Jam* and I watch Netflix now as a way to relax at home when I get some peace and quiet. I don't exercise as much as I used to. I can go for a run for 45 minutes and just plod along, and with my heart monitor on, I know how hard to push myself. Chantelle and I used to run together, when she was training for the Great North Run, and I enjoyed that, but we haven't made the time to do that recently.

I was very young when I first became a father. I met Kylee, my ex, as most young people did back then before Tinder, in a nightclub at the age of 18, and two years later we had our first child, Jamaal. A year after that, we had another son, Micah, and then three years later we had a daughter, Liyah. Looking back, we were probably too young to have kids. We didn't know anything about life or about parenting. She was 19 and I was 20. We were in Leicester and my football career was taking off. It was a case of sink or swim, and we swam.

From experience, it was very tough. I know more about my kids now than I did with the kids I had when I was younger.

I get to do stuff now with my kids that I couldn't back then. I'd be in hotels away from them, and at tournaments with England in the summer. Now, I wash the little ones, make their breakfast, and help them get ready for their day. It's totally different, but that's the way life is. It changes.

I have four children with Chantelle: Jaden, Reigan, Milanna and Mendes and they all live with us in the North West, with Jamaal, Micah and Liyah living with their mum, Kylee, in Leicester. All our children are in contact, which is nice. The age gap is difficult, but they speak and have contact. Jaden, who is my eldest with Chan, would always look up to his big brothers and follow them around when he was little. It's a lovely memory I'll always cherish.

* * *

My relationship with Kylee was great; we had children together and we were happy. It was different though, as we were so young. Kylee came to Liverpool with me after I left Leicester and we were a family all together. They followed soon after I'd moved out of the hotel and into our apartment. I was still young at Liverpool in terms of my maturity too. Sometimes relationships just drift, and I want to say it was nothing to do with Kylee. I met Chantelle. I wasn't out there looking for girls, I just met someone and fell in love with her.

Chan has a similar character to me. She is relaxed; we can both be a little too laid-back at times to be honest. As laid-back as we are, I'm not just sat on the couch though. We're both working, keeping busy and we support each other. If

Chan is out at the restaurant, then I'm with the kids. We're a team, working together for our family.

The kids play so much sport, which keeps them active and if you don't do that, they'll be on an iPad all the time, which isn't good. My daughter, Milanna, could pick up my iPad from the age of 18 months and would find what she wanted on YouTube within seconds. We've had them playing lacrosse, karate, football, everything. Some of that comes from my sporting background, but it's Chan really who has instilled that into them. She was driving through Wilmslow one day and saw some kids playing football. She pulled the car over and introduced herself to the football coaches and asked what age they could start at, which was six.

Jaden was only four, but was big for his age. They accepted him and then asked if he would enrol at Manchester City a few years later. At first, as I hadn't seen him play, I watched and said to Chan we needed to pull him out as he was too far behind. I didn't want him in that situation. I didn't realise that the kids were two years older than him. Within three months he had caught up and then surpassed some of them. He was also training with Liverpool, and was in his Villa kit as I was playing for them at the time.

Then we took Reigan along to training, just so he could run around at the age of two, as he wasn't old enough to take part, but there he was, chasing after people and trying to get the ball. It must be in the genes. Reigan joined Manchester City's academy as well, and the most important thing is that they both enjoy it. Sometimes, he'll say he doesn't want to go and wants to spend time with his mates, or be at home, and I'm fine with that. I don't want them to feel any pressure to play. If you're forcing someone to play football, it's not right. Now they're older, they make their own minds up.

If you asked my kids, I think they'd say that I'm a tough father. I'm a softer version of my dad. My kids get away with a lot, and my dad is really soft with them too, as that's how grandads are. I think it's good that I'm strict and then Chan will use my name to ensure the kids behave, otherwise I'll get involved. Chan is tough too, but she's very playful and loving with them. She will joke with Reigan all the time. He's such a character and he will stall before going to bed, trying to stay up as long as he can. It always makes me laugh.

I see a lot of me in Jaden as a character; he's calm, organised and easy-going. Micah is the spitting image of me to look at though. I will be honest and say that I just wanted them to be happy. I didn't want them to go into football necessarily, and be labelled as Heskey's kids. If they choose that path, then that's fine with me. They could always put their first name on the back of their shirt if they make it, but people will still compare them to me. I just want what's best for them. I didn't want the stigma that comes with being my kids and being a footballer.

It's great that Jaden and Reigan are getting the experience of travelling as well as playing, so that will help them to develop as people. Jamaal went to university and studied economics, which is a great achievement too. I should have pushed my older kids more though, but I was so involved in football and so young myself. I am proud of them all though, and they will all make their own choices. I never got the chance to be a kid like my mates did, as football took over, so I hope they continue to forge their own lives and be happy and successful.

Chantelle and I understand each other and that's so important. We're best friends as well. We confide in each other and that's so important.

I'm at my happiest being there for my family, being relaxed and being at home. That's my life now. For so long, it was just about my career, and now it's about others and that makes me content. Happiness is about being comfortable with who you are and everything around you.

Sometimes, I will head off on my own for a walk, through the local parks or golf courses, hat on and head down, near to where we live and I will clear my head, get some fresh air and feel good about life. I love going away to Antigua to see my parents as well. It's a shame they don't live nearer to us, as they would love to be with the grandkids more, but then it does mean we get to have incredible, quality time in the Caribbean with them, creating memories.

I used to send my eldest kids over when I was playing, and although we don't get to see them as often as we would like, we get out there once a year if we can. My parents have land that they farm, and they have a two-hour walk in the morning. The weather is amazing and their lifestyle is what they want. They also come back once a year but we stay in touch on WhatsApp video, so they don't lose contact with us and the kids.

Family is important to me. It's everything. I want to be there for my family and I want them to know that I would do anything for them. Chan, my parents and my children are my world. I'm looking forward to what the future will bring for us all.

CHAPTER FOURTEEN

We Can Talk, but it's Time to Act

LEICESTER is often described as a multicultural city and a cohesive community. A mixture of white, black and Asian people, but in truth we only generally mix in the city centre. There are areas where races of people live and a few exceptions where races mix.

When I was growing up, I can honestly say that I didn't know much about white culture as I wasn't exposed to it until I left Highfields and went to Evington and to junior school at Linden. In Highfields, when we went to the pub it was a black pub, the video shop was run by an Asian family and the chip shop was owned by a black guy. We only had reggae and calypso music on in the pub and dominoes were played on the tables. That was my experience. I noticed, from a young age, that in certain communities people would stare at me. It was the 1980s and I wasn't stupid. I would hear things being said about me and I sensed the looks. I had been sheltered from this within Highfields. As I grew older, I visited other places and I had to develop a thick skin. It became the norm, but it shouldn't have been. It wasn't nice for a kid, but it must have been much worse for my family when they moved over to the UK. They were told they couldn't rent a certain house, or go into places, just because they were black. Now, my dad was a fighter, that was his character and he and his friends stuck together and did what they had to do to survive. That helped to make things easier for us as kids.

When I was racially abused as a youngster near to Filbert Street, all they knew was that I was black and I was a Leicester City supporter. They had no clue that I was about to become the team's centre-forward and that within a couple of years they would be cheering for me from the stands. Racism is a blind spot for people. It's something that takes them over, even down to the point that as a young kid I knew if I saw a group of white lads ahead of me, I would have to be aware and either walk through them or cross the road.

I look at my kids now and they don't think that way, which I'm grateful for. Racism hasn't disappeared. It manifests in different ways. I'll give you an example. I will walk down the streets around where I live in Cheshire, and be asked if I'm a footballer. The assumption that for me to live in a nice suburban area, as a black man, must mean I am an athlete of some sort, is something I find very strange. Who would ask that of someone? Who would even think it? I could have been successful in business, but people look at people and make immediate judgements and distinctions.

When I was younger, I would go into nightclubs and often be asked by people if I had any drugs to sell. There is no doubt in my mind that was because I was black. I've never taken drugs in my life, so what on earth would possess them to ask something like that, apart from racial stereotyping? What says to you that I am a drug dealer? I don't know how people dared ask me that. John Barnes has touched upon these stereotypes; like if you are Jamaican, you are seen as a Yardie, a drug dealer. A Muslim is seen as a terrorist threat, a Nigerian is seen as a scam artist. That is the impression that the media portray and that seeps into society. That is desperately dangerous in my eyes.

Although it's not as well documented, we also have colourism within the black community, between people who have darker- and lighter-coloured skin. Lighter is always seen as better. If you have coarse hair that is seen as worse as well. There are people who use a bleaching agent within body creams to lighten their skin tone. It is sold widely and I can't believe that they would be safe to use. You have dark-skinned people walking around with umbrellas to avoid the sunlight. Even people I know will comment on skin tone. I've had people close to me say, 'Ain't you dark?' and while you don't think about it at the time, I remember it as a kid and the way being defined by my colour has affected me. I didn't like it.

Then there was the normalisation of terms like, 'When are we going round to Black Dave's?' It is very strange to me when I think back and imagine people saying that. You wouldn't say, 'When are we going round to White Sandra's?' would you? Both examples would stand out today and would be offensive, which at least shows some progress.

I only experienced outward, obvious racism a few times on the football field as a youth player. I would hear the sniggers from people on the sidelines, and would hear them question whether I was too old to play due to my size and athleticism. I had a couple of growth spurts, at age 10 and then again at 15. I couldn't control my size. My mum's side of the family were huge; size 12 feet, tall and stocky. I just got my head down and tried to block out any comments. I think those comments and assumptions still happen today.

How much can you withstand? How much racism can you take as an individual until you react? At youth level, in one particular game, my team-mate and I were abused throughout the game by a couple of opponents. Eventually, after being called all sorts of things, my team-mate ended it by knocking them both out.

Everyone has a limit. It wasn't subtle either. Everyone could hear what they were saying, but no one reacted, said anything or tried to stop it. We were just told to get on with the game and stop moaning. But why should we have to put up with that? Being called a nigger over and over again was not acceptable.

As a black person, I always felt that we were at the bottom of the pile in society. I didn't feel like I was personally, but that's how our race has been treated. It's a deeper issue than just me, but it's something I've never been able to understand. I've got friends who have put job applications in, knowing that they won't get the role because of their colour. I can see that my life would have been a lot tougher if I wasn't a footballer. I'd have probably ended up in a factory job and would have experienced racism face-to-face.

The black community used to just work to survive, but now there are black people progressing within sport and the business community, so that is a positive. There needs to be black role models in all industries too. In football, there's John Barnes, Chris Powell, Chris Hughton and Les Ferdinand, but there needs to be more, not the same names. We need to see black people earning key roles within the business community in order to inspire young kids to follow them, in the same way that I looked up to John Barnes in football.

There's only so much that football can do. Clubs and governing bodies are doing well, but they can only do so much. Racism is an issue for society, not just for football. I grew up with a lot of Asian friends who were very good at football, extremely talented, but they were written off as not having the character to make it as a footballer, so they didn't. If you tell someone they aren't good enough, enough times, then eventually they will believe you. It is just plain wrong.

I don't know where we are at with racism in the game now. In the 1980s it was blatant. Now, it is still there, but is hidden away. Is that better? No. Racism is racism, whatever form it comes in. You can walk into a stadium now and not hear a single racist comment, as people are risking prosecution, but that doesn't mean it's eradicated. It is down to education. Kids are not born with hate in their hearts, they are taught to hate. Growing up, if I was called a 'black bastard', I'd either have to take it on the chin, or fight them. I couldn't report it as nothing would be done, and the chances are the authorities would side with the aggressor.

These kinds of incidents were part and parcel of being a young black man. Now, people have to respect the laws, which is a positive, but those views still exist. That is the worry. How do we solve that problem? How do you deal with a hate crime?

I played with a white player during my professional career that harboured racist views at one stage, as a result of being chased and attacked by a group of black people when he was younger. He changed those views after becoming best friends with a black player. He realised that not all black people were evil. His views were wrong, but he has educated himself and listened to the people around him who were trying to help.

In society, as I've already said, we pigeon-hole people. Black people are always classed as lazy, so therefore, if you meet a black person you think they are lazy. What evidence is there of this stereotype? Were black people not the slaves in the past, doing all the hard, manual labour in awful conditions? It is time for people to treat each other as individuals and to help educate each other. We have a responsibility to make sure our children create a more positive, inclusive world and to break down these disgusting stereotypes and hateful attitudes.

What can football do to help solve the issue of racism? Football brings everyone together. We find common ground to support the same team as one. As players at youth level, right the way through to veterans, we unite to try to beat the opposition and we celebrate or commiserate together, regardless of our colour or creed. There is more that unites us than divides us, and that's the power of football.

Society sees people live and die in the same area, never changing their views and never meeting new people, forming prejudicial opinions about the world, without actually experiencing anything first-hand.

While playing for Leicester, I went out to a pub in Braunstone with some friends of mine and we sat down for a drink. Within moments, we were told by someone we knew that we had to leave. We knew why. We were all black. We just finished our drinks and left. It was people within the pub who asked us to leave, not those that owned or ran the place. It was an example of bigoted people who didn't want their local pub to change. Football can take you out of that comfort zone, so it can be a positive. Racism is a problem within football, but it is far from being exclusively football's problem.

Take the media for example. The way young black footballers have been covered within tabloid newspapers is awful. The headlines are written to incite hatred and jealously against black players, but are complimentary to white players. It is a simple manipulation and it has been happening for a long time. The sooner the public reject this form of media and find out the truth for themselves, the better.

I've seen Ashley Cole, England's best-ever left-back, mark someone out of a game and then be rated as four out of ten in the paper. People may say it's nothing to do with colour, but there was open hatred towards Ashley; for him taking a better salary at Chelsea than the one he was on at Arsenal, and he went on to win lots of trophies, justifying his decision. Many white players have done the same in their careers but they didn't receive the hate that he did.

The media's manipulation of people's views was never more evident than through Brexit. The xenophobic narrative which was spread by the media and those leading the leave campaign, has been shown for what it is – lies. We don't appreciate how powerful the media is. It's where we receive all of our information from and it helps to form our opinions and our voice about anything and everything. Social media can help against the manipulation, as footballers, for example, can directly communicate with the public, but that is just one outlet. The mainstream media is still dangerously powerful. I should know as I have been attacked and ridiculed too many times to count.

Organisations like Kick It Out can only do so much. They bring awareness and they work hard with a limited budget. They have had difficulties in the past and have clashed with players too, but they are a not-for-profit company, in a world of very big fish.

If I'm honest, I'm not sure if the FA know what to do about racism within the game. It is too large an issue for them to solve on their own. How can a group of older, white men tell me, or anyone else who has suffered from racism, how to resolve the issue? They can't. They don't have the experience to deal with this. The FA needs greater diversity, and needs to speak to people who have suffered to find out how it feels to be treated like that. Then they need to empower those people to action real change within the game.

I've seen television debates about racism with white people speaking about it. I don't want to sound prejudiced myself, but what are they going to add to the debate? We need people to make change happen. I acknowledge that it's difficult for the FA, but there are many of us around who would help if we were approached.

Something which really gets to me is that there is so much talk about racism, so much awareness these days, and yet it still exists and at times to me, it feels as if nothing is being done. That's how I feel. We are a nation of talkers. I want to see some action. I want to see a time where racism doesn't exist. I want to see people being educated. In football, I want to see a committee of ex-players, managers and current players, empowered to eradicate it. Knowing how things are done though, it would take years of arguing over what the committee would do and who would sit on it.